FIND YOUR TRUE VOICE
YOUR WEAKNESS LIGHTS THE WAY

CHRIS TAYLOR, Ph.D.

Find Your True Voice
by Chris Taylor

Copyright © 2021 by Chris Taylor

Printed in the United States of America

Bridgework Publishing
P.O. Box 382734
Birmingham, Alabama 35238

ISBN: 978-1-7370238-0-7

For Worldwide Distribution
Printed in the U.S.A.

1. The main category of the book — Non Fiction, Psychology, Human Development, Career guidance, Stuttering, life transitions.

First Edition
10 9 8 7 6 5 4 3 2 1

DEDICATION

I dedicate this to my wife, Faith, without whose love, encouragement, sacrifice and patience, this book would not have been completed; to my three children, Will who has taught me how to fight the good fight and protect the family; To Grace who has taught me to run the race of life with confidence and help those in need; to Zach who has shown me a leader makes commitments and cares; and lastly, I dedicate this to my mother, Betty, who shown me the power of unconditional love.

In Memory of my friend
Rob Rayborn
9/22/65-3/25/21

CONTENT

INTRODUCTION

The Obstacle Became the way

"We forget: In life, it doesn't matter what happens to you or where you came from. It matters what you do with what happens and what you've been given."

— Ryan Holiday
(Author : The Obstacle Is The Way)

We spend much of our lives trying to avoid problems or obstacles. Very rarely do we become aware that our obstacle or impediment may be the most important clue of our destiny and passion. I mean how could something blocking our path help us? We are taught by life that it is strength that makes us great, not our weakness. Strong people can lift heavy weights, get the admiration of others, and dispel a since of inadequacy. Everyone wants to be known for their strength in the face of challenge. Those that score highest on test, or run the fastest on a field, or make the most money, are seen as being the worthiest of admiration.

A peanuts cartoon from the peanuts comic strip of the 1950's shows adventures of Charlie Brown. Lucy in the comic strip asked Charlie Brown why he was looking so gloom or sad. Charlie Brown says "I feel inferior." "Oh" says Lucy, "you shouldn't worry about that. Lots of people have that feeling." "What that their inferior?" Charlie Brown asks. "No," Lucy replies. "that you're Inferior." This play on words emphasizes the idea that being weak, or inferior is not desirable. It shows that people who rightly or wrongly think themselves strong can rub in and mock a since of weakness that others have. No one wants to be a weak person or weak leader. But what if you could find in your hurdle or weakness your greatest benefit? What if you could find in your flaw, or your impediment that secret power available only to you? For superman, his weak-ness was Kryptonite. But what if he could harness the power of Kryptonite and make it work for him and not against him? It is a paradox to think of weakness as a strength. How can a weakness bring us strength? I say that our weakness lays the groundwork for our strength.

Everyone wants to be heard or seen by others and not ignored or pitied. When people are paralyzed by what they see as weakness or an impediment, they can withdraw into the shadows. To not have a voice is like slowly dying alone in the dark. When we do not have a voice, it is hard to care for other people and it is hard to feel secure in the world. Having a voice is having a place of personal significance in the world. The word vocation is rooted in the Latin word "voice." I like how Frederick Buechner (1993) defines vocation as,

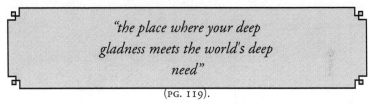

"the place where your deep gladness meets the world's deep need"

(PG. 119).

Often people do not let their voice speak because they feel like a nobody, an outcast, or a misfit in the crowd. Life often beats out of us any since of calling or purpose in the world. The silver lining in this book is that there is hope. You must find the role in your story that you were meant to play. You are more than you have become if you are not confident in your voice. I am calling you to discover your own hero's journey in these pages. You must let your voice speak by finding your voice in a noisy world. Many people cannot hear their own voice because all the other voices in their lives are louder than theirs. Voices from our past saying we are not enough. Voices in our present saying we are not worthy. Many times, we are just plain afraid of our own voice being either too weak or too strong. If it is too weak than we might be rejected or ignored. If it is too strong or unique, we might feel we would not fit in with the crowd and we could be rejected. It is like singing in a group, and not knowing how good or how bad you might sound. For many it is just easier to fit in and not be too weak or too strong. The next quote by Marianne Williamson speaks of a tug of war that we often have inside of ourselves as we relate to the world, and it also represents the challenge I make in this book, *"We are born to make manifest the Glory of God that is within us."*

"Our deepest fear is not that we are inadequate, our deepest fear is that we are more powerful beyond measure. It is our light, not our darkness that most frightens us. We ask ourselves who am I to be brilliant, gorgeous, talented, fabulous? Actually, who are you not to be? You are a child of God. You're playing small does not serve the world. There is nothing enlightened about shrinking so that other people won't feel insecure around you. We were born to make manifest the glory of God that is within us. It is not just in some of us; it is in everyone. And as we let our own light shine, we unconsciously give other people permission to do the same. As we are liberated from our own fear, our presence automatically liberates others."

— MARIANNE WILLIAMSON

I want you to find your voice and let it speak because the world needs your voice. The voice includes both our strengths and our weaknesses. To find our authentic voice we must embrace both that part of ourselves which we feel confident about and that part of our self with which we feel inadequate or weak. It is my hope that in your journey through this book and story you will begin to embrace your true voice.

ABOUT THIS BOOK

What is in it and Who is this guy?

Over the course of my life—more times than I can count—I have searched for my voice, and it just wasn't there. One of my traits that people identify with me is stuttering. Stuttering feels like having a mark on you like a scarlet letter. The mark gave me the deep since of being a misfit. To start out in life feeling like you are not enough, never completely goes away. The downside early on was in the false mask I wore to try to hide my speech impediment. In hiding my flaw, I was denying my true self and a deeper gift I have to offer the world. Simply put, I now know that my weakness is the way. The way for me has been most refined in the obstacle of my speech impediment. I believe the way of satisfaction in life and career is in the struggle, pain, weakness, or obstacle that makes us the most human and sometimes the most true to our self. We need to know our story deep enough to find our voice.

I've always had a speech impediment. I used to call girls on the phone, but I had so much trouble. They would hang up on me before I could ever get a word out. This left me feeling very defeated.

My story is not only about stuttering, per say, but the search to find a purpose for life. I would often ask the question "Why am I here?" It did not make since to me to struggle so hard to communicate. It did not make since to me to have people look away from me when I spoke, as if to pretend they did not see my struggle or that they did not know how to respond to my struggle.

My stuttering has caused me to run with a little more weight in life, but that very weight strengthened me and showed me the way the more I understood my story.

Most of us know we are not perfect. We all have some form of deficiency that keeps us from our image of perfection. Whether it is a character flaw or physical disability, we all have something we aren't proud of—something that makes us so uncomfortable that our confidence levels plummet to zero whenever we think about it, or it becomes obvious to the people we want to impress.

Part of my motivation to write this book comes from a story I experienced where someone acknowledged my voice. It was a cold winter day on the playground at Fountain Lake elementary school. The teachers always let us go outside and run around during third period. Everyone had their group they hung around with, and, for the most part, I tried to get along with every group.

There was one group that seemed a little like the outsiders of the school. We called them the "druggies." I do not know if they really took drugs or not. In my memory, they dressed in mostly black clothes and smelled like cigarette smoke. That day, I tried to connect with them in a friendly "hello," but one of them started to mock my stuttering while imitating my facial expressions when I spoke. This went on for a few minutes and was very painful for me.

Out of nowhere, the respected leader of the group, and maybe all groups, stepped in. His name was Todd, and he was tougher and larger than most. He said to the guys mocking me, "No more. He's my friend and if you mess with him, you mess with me!" The boys immediately backed off.

I will never forget Todd because he made me feel like I was worth something. He made me feel I had a voice. That is what I want to do for my readers. I want to step in and help you to have a voice like Todd did for me. Todd told me I belonged, and I was worth something.

In this book, I want to give you the motivation to turn hindrances and adversity into courage and strength. I am a stutterer and now a public speaker. I got an eleven out of a possible thirty-six on the college entrance exam (ACT) and was given very little chance to succeed in college, but I now have a Ph.D. in Educational Psychology. I use to shy away from speaking in public but now I welcome the opportunity to release the same strength that has come from my struggle.

Whether your personal challenge, weakness, or struggle is related to being overweight, underweight, shy, tall, short, non-athletic, school challenged, or a stutterer, embrace your potential for a secret power in your unique message. Whatever your perceived weakness, or challenge, you don't have to hide it. If you try to hide it, you are likely cutting yourself off from the very ability that makes you powerful.

One way to think about weakness is to look at it a little closer. The struggle, or experience, in your life making you feel vulnerable when seen by other people made you who you are today. You either have tried to cover it up and live from a false self or you embraced it and used it to guide you to your true voice. I want to make sure you are aware of that story so you can be your best self as you move forward.

My personal battle with communication has made me work hard to communicate a deeper message to people about the purpose and meaning of life. I had a friend tell me she felt overweight, and it had been a struggle her whole life. What if she embraced her struggle with weight to find her most authentic self? What if her struggle was to empower her rather than lead her to shame? What if she could view her weakness as her deepest message and source of strength to connect to people? The more she tried to hide it, the more power it held over her. I can now report that when she changed her mindset about her weight—and the more she embraced her weight as a vulnerability—the greater her connection to herself and to the world became. The world wants real, authentic individuals, not the airbrushed photographs.

As someone who stutters, I spent a lot of energy trying to hide my struggle with things like cars, sports, clothes, weight-lifting and college degrees. All good things and important for that stage of my journey, but the danger is in believing those external things were who I had to become in order to be accepted by others. I felt if I could present myself as successful or cool, I would be seen as "normal", rather than flawed.

I didn't want anyone to see my weakness, so my effort became a mask to cover my insecurity. Deep down I'd always felt that by hiding, no one could hurt me. I saw my speech as an ugly part of myself.

As you will hear in my story, my journey led me to this quote from the Bible:

"My grace is sufficient for you, for My power is made perfect in your weakness. I will boast all the more gladly in weakness"

(2 Corinthians 12:9 [NIV]).

Can you boast in your weakness or struggle, or are you afraid to be seen? You must view your weakness as a gift.

Shame researcher Brené Brown says, "Vulnerability is about showing up and being seen. It's tough to do that when we're terrified about what people might see or think."

As I share my journey with you, I hope you can find rest for your soul and the strength to be more authentic as you let yourself be seen.

I have broken this book into a three-part journey of the *actor* voice, *achiever* voice, and *author* voice. In Section 1, the actor is mostly assigned positions early on in life by parents, teachers, coaches, and other important role models. The actor is often acting with no clear view or awareness of his or her own goals but to please the person who assigns them positions on the field or stage. The main goal for an actor is to please others. If you look, you can identify people in society that work a job with no real enjoyment or goal, but to survive. Pleasing others only causes people to eventually lose their identity.

The second section of the journey is the achiever voice. The achiever has more focus and control over the hurdles he or she wants to jump over with a better view of the personal goal. The achiever is still focused on survival but with more feeling of control over the outcome. The achiever can be a person in a career wanting to rise to the top and achieve success with a plan to do so. Many of my students that focus on achieving an "A" on a test, often do not focus on understanding for the sake of true learning.

My final third section, the author voice, is about a deeper awareness of the internal motivations through one's story. A good author can tell a story and be aware of the hidden message below the surface of the script or movie. Everyone knows something about storytelling, but accomplished authors know what the deeper message is of the story. Let's begin your journey to learn your author voice.

SECTION 1

Actor Voice

CHAPTER 1

Fear of Never Being Anything

"I could hardly talk. It took me three minutes to complete a sentence. It was crushing for anyone who wanted to express themselves, who wanted to be heard and couldn't. It was frightening. Yet, when I became another character, in a play, I lost the stutter. It was phenomenal."

BRUCE WILLIS
(ACTOR AND STUTTERER)

When I was fifteen years old, I worked at my dad's hardware store during the summer, and for fifty-five years, there is one moment that impacts me still to this day. One day, a former military man and friend of my dad's came in. Colonel James Harwood was a high-ranking officer in the military and had retired in our community of Fountain Lake,

Arkansas. Fountain Lake was a suburb outside the city of Hot Springs, Arkansas. We did not consider ourselves city folks. Fountain Lake could be described as a rural area with more blue-collar workers. Colonel Harwood was considered a form of a hero to our community. He seemed to have a broader knowledge of the world. My dad really respected him. When Jim came in the store that day, my dad asked,

"Hi, Jim! What are you working on today?"

"I need an electrical plug," Jim responded.

"My son can show you where the plugs are," my dad quickly responded.

The colonel put his hand out. "Hi, I'm Jim Harwood," he said.

"I am C-C-C-C-C-Chris," I said, shaking his hand.

For a stutterer like myself, saying my name was the hardest. It was like it is somehow connected to a unique word that represented one's identity and that moment when people will make a first impression of you. During that moment, I thought I would pass out. It felt like an eternity before I got my name out. I felt the shame in embarrassing myself and my dad, who I wanted to make proud and show I could be a man.

"Good to meet you, young man," Jim said after I finally said my name. I then showed him where the electrical plugs were.

After Jim left, my dad pulled me aside. "Chris, you have to overcome that stuttering," he said. My dad was a role model, and always a powerful voice in my life. He was the voice of reason when I needed it. He was my support when I was down. He was the one person I looked up to no matter what. So, you could imagine my feelings when he said,

> *"Chris, you will never be anything*
> *as long as you stutter."*

Those ten words have impacted my life so much. In hindsight, I understand my dad better now that I'm older. I know he wanted to help me so I could make it in the world.

Many people from my area come from a line of practical blue-collar laborers, truck or bus drivers, electricians, and store owners. These types of service-oriented people make up the backbone of many small-town communities in the south. I came from a culture where discussing your feelings wasn't a normal topic of discussion. To people in a small town like mine, a broken leg was easier to acknowledge, than a shame-filled heart. In our little community, a medical doctor has more esteem than a college professor or a writer, and not everyone gets a trophy for participating. There were only winners and losers. In rural communities like the one I came from, philosophical ideas have less value to people than surviving and providing the basic needs of life like food, shelter, health, clothing, and serving the community.

At the time, my mind caused me to think the worst. *This stuttering is a curse. It is keeping me from being myself or being useful to the world. My dad says I will never be anything. I will never be accepted as long as I have this stutter.* This lie I was telling myself has been a driving force for much of my life. I kept telling myself I needed to be someone else if I wanted to be accepted in the world.

Early events can either defeat you or make you stronger. These moments are like villains in a movie that steal your youthful innocence and show you the world is much harsher than you believed. However, a villain can also show your purpose for life. Your most challenging memories can give you a clue to something underneath the surface that can help teach you how to listen.

My dad never shied away from verbal confrontations. He was physically tough and an electrician by trade. He could fix anything that was broken, except me. He was a provider and protector, taking on challenges no matter how big they were. At times, I believed his strength could bend people like he could bend a piece of electrical pipe. One angry look on his face would send fear through me. I never saw my dad as the villain because I only saw him as the hero and protector, I knew he was. I wanted to make him proud and show him I was more than someone who needed to be fixed.

The quest to prove yourself usually begins with the attempt to be seen and valued in some areas of early life. The stage was set for me to change my image from what I saw as broken, flawed, and embarrassing, to something I felt would be more respected, strong, and successful. The problem was that I changed on the surface, but that kind of change does not always heal the emotional struggle inside. This was when I developed my first mask to hide both my weakness and feelings of shame. Masking is a term used in psychology as concealing one's emotion by portraying another emotion. We wear a mask to hide our vulnerabilities, weakness, and pain. We behave in a way that does not expose our perceived weakness to the world by overcompensating with strength. Many times, men are told to stop crying like a girl or stop being emotional. The message we got was "men must be strong." My dad would say to me when I was very young, "Give me some of those tears." Even to talk about this makes me cringe. You might be thinking I am emotional, and you might interpret that as weak. Trust me, I learned to hide or stuff my emotions deep inside myself. I cannot remember crying in my twenties.

When I heard those words from my dad, "Chris, you will never be anything as long as you stutter," I unconsciously decided to protect myself by hiding the pain of feeling shame.

In my teen years, I was constantly seeking acceptance, approval, and love from everyone in my life. The shame I felt from stuttering caused me to want to hide my inner self with a more external self. It was a form of disconnection from where the pain was and an attempt to find acceptance and love. I began placing more emphasis on my external strengths like football, cars, clothes, and running fast.

I became achievement focused. I used it as a form of self-protection. I was learning I could get the recognition I wanted by doing things like running the forty-yard dash in 4.5 seconds, building my body to be more muscular, and driving a cool car.

Early performances on life's stage begin to create an identity or voice for most teenagers. I use the word "voice" as another representation of identity or self.

By my senior year, I started to feel pretty good about myself. I was selected to be the principal for a day through the beta club and picked by cheerleaders to be homecoming king in a mock homecoming. In my senior year, I was muscular and the starting defensive back for the football team. I drove a four-wheel-drive Jeep Renegade with a big, tough winch on the front. I was the lifeguard at the local country club. I got a great tan that summer.

I do not remember much about my feelings during this time. Everything was like an outward performance on an actor's stage. I was mostly concerned with my image and getting girls to like me.

Early on, you're often taught to listen to everyone else's voice but your own in an effort to get approval of others. You can become more focused on performances to obtain external praise rather than on recognizing and developing your true self.

The desire to perform shows up in people of all ages. I remember when my oldest son Will was twenty-one, he appeared to be losing hope over being the golden boy of his high school. I could tell he was not where he wished to be in his career, with money, or even a romantic relationship. My friends kept telling me I had to let my son work through his struggles and be there for him in any way I could.

"I do not know what I am fighting for."

In the depths of his struggle, my son said this to me. Listening to his heartbreak, I recalled the many times I felt the same way, although it took me longer to admit it to myself. My own personal identity crisis became evident as I struggled to make my path perfect. Perhaps that's why those words felt so painful to hear. I didn't want him to struggle with his identity as I had with mine, but I think it is a part of the youthful journey. To watch my oldest son, go through these challenges had been another layer of painful growth for myself that I didn't know I could experience. That's when I discovered that people learn most in the crisis of their identity.

A parent's instinct is to pick their children up when they fall down or struggle. In return, the child then looks up to see how their parent reacts to their falling down. If a parent looks terrified after a fall, the child will take on the same emotion.

This raised my deepest fear and pain. The boy I had picked up when he fell was now beyond the scope of my parental ability beyond just listening to him. I felt helpless being lost on how to save him through his difficulties. The truth is my fear and worry were embarrassing to him. I know now my son only wanted me to be there for him and listen. He just needed to tell me about the struggles he was going through without me trying to fix him.

Perhaps that was what my dad felt when he saw my struggle to speak when I was my son's age.

I remember like it was yesterday. My son told me in a moment of humility, "I don't have a job, money, or a girl. I don't even have the ability to help and save others like I want to." Like my son, I have spent my life trying to help and save others, but I have learned that others are most helped when I am vulnerable about my own story and struggles. Young people as well as older need to know they are not alone in the pain. They also need to be heard but not always rescued from the struggle. It is in this struggle that we all are most prepared for larger challenges in life.

I have felt so much of what my son felt. In my twenties, I wanted to save people, and I think I still do. I wished I had more money, and I believed I should have been farther along than I was. On my bad days, I believed other people had it easier than me.

In some ways, I still struggle with these thoughts.

Years ago, I had less awareness of what the phrase "never be anything" meant, but it sounded, inside my own head, like my life would not matter if I could not overcome the stuttering. In a town of hard-working people, to matter meant to serve and make a contribution to the practical visual needs of people. A medical doctor, a schoolteacher, a high-ranking military officer, a lawyer, or a small business owner would rank highest in my little community. Because of that, my dad was in favor of me going to college so I would not have to work as hard as he did.

If you have been driven most of your life by a core fear or a core traumatic memory, I want you to try to define it.

Doing this will help you to find the true self hiding in the shadows behind the mask. Your pain can be your friend if it shows you the path to fulfillment and purpose.

CHAPTER 2

Finding Strength in Weakness

Finding Strength

*An inevitable and often ignored dimension of the quest
for 'wholeness' is that we must embrace what we dislike
or find shameful about ourselves as well as what
we are confident and proud of.*

PARKER PALMER

It has often seemed like there were two sides of me begging for attention. Early on in my life, I tried to ignore the side of me that felt weak or embarrassing. One side of me wanted to show the world I wasn't a failure through achievements, while the other side wanted to relate better to those similar to me and who needed encouragement.

I used to love the animated *Rudolph, the Red-Nosed Reindeer* reruns. They wouldn't let him join in any reindeer games, so Rudolph left home to find acceptance with other misfits. Later in life, Rudolph decided to return home, and when a blizzard hits on Christmas Eve, the "weakness" that made him leave in the first place became a unique and useful gift! Santa turned to Rudolph and asked, "Rudolph, with your nose so bright, will you guide my sleigh tonight?"

That part of Rudolph, the part of himself that he felt shameful about and tried to hide, became the part that gave him the uniqueness which saved Christmas. I can relate to that. That part of me I wanted to hide and get rid of did not go away for me but has now become the strong light to show others the way and most of all God's power in my weakness.

There were conflicting voices I could hear going on inside of me. For example, there was a girl named Donna in elementary school who had holes in her clothes. Some of my friends always made fun of her. I felt conflicted as I joined in on their laughing and teasing, giving her a misfit ranking, though I feared being a misfit as well. Despite my focus on being accepted by my peers, a strange sadness filled me when I thought about the things she lacked in her life, like proper clothes or friends to support her. Deep down, I felt I was a misfit like her. It scared me because I knew I was like Donna, but I was able to disguise my struggle behind my mask. I felt a connection with her, but I did nothing about it, and soon the feeling disappeared. I didn't want to feel sadness for Donna because it reminded me of my own, so I buried it out of shame. These kinds of conflicting voices are part of the development for most preteen and early teenagers.

Many teenagers either believe they are always on stage and being watched and at the same time feel like no one sees them for who they truly are. I had the feeling I was behind a curtain and no one could see me until I did something extraordinary, then people seemed to notice. Today with the presence of social media like Facebook and Instagram, it is worse for youth to have their identity tied to the number of likes they get after posting a picture, video, or status update. What if they do not get many likes? Many times their self-esteem is affected.

There was a battle between the two ways I viewed myself. I felt either noticed and valued, or invisible and pitied. I was on the search for significance. One of the tasks for an adolescent with healthy growth is to bring the parts of themselves into a unified whole. A divided self is like the difference between the onstage actor and their true character off stage. As a teenager, I did not have the words to express or understand what was going on inside of me, so I often hide behind the curtain of life.

The world I grew up in taught boys that emotions and feelings are a weakness and make you vulnerable, which I believe still exists today. Showing certain kinds of emotion on the football field and in many other working environments is not acceptable. Crying because you feel weak or afraid is unacceptable, especially for men. Boys are often told to "stop crying if you want to be a man and not a girl." Because of this, many men cannot describe what they or others are feeling very well. We can learn to disconnect from our hearts.

An example of the need for men to connect to their hearts is the words of former American Psychology Association President, Ron Levant, who gave the condition a name, normative male alexithymia. In an article in *Psychology Today* (Henriques, 2014), normative male alexithymia refers to the traditional masculine role of socialization channeling men's actual emotions through their own masculine identity into what they feel they are "allowed" to express (i.e. they will be shamed and will feel as if they are not "real men" if they express feelings of vulnerability, dependency, or weakness).

Boys aren't the only ones who were taught to conform to culture; girls also have these internal voices telling them to be someone else to be accepted.

The website Everyday Sexism Project (2012) received this deeply moving entry from a fifteen-year-old girl. She wrote:

I'm fifteen and feel like girls my age are under a lot of pressure ... I always feel like if I don't look a certain way, if boys don't think I'm 'sexy' or 'hot,' then I've failed and it doesn't even matter if I am a doctor or writer, I'll still feel like nothing ... successful women are only considered a success if they are successful *and* hot, and I worry constantly that I won't be. What if my boobs don't grow? What if I don't have the perfect body? What if my hips don't widen and give me a little waist? If none of that happens, I feel like [sic] there's no point in doing anything because I'll just be the 'fat ugly girl' regardless of whether I do become a doctor or not.

This young girl embodies the struggle that everyone goes through. Society and culture have taught children to believe they are never going to be enough unless they look and act a certain way. I like the quote by EE Cummings:

"To be nobody-but-yourself—in a world which is doing its best, night and day, to make you everybody but yourself—means to fight the hardest battle which any human being can fight; and never stop fighting."

David Brooks gives a perspective on the conflict or division in ourselves. He identifies résumé and eulogy virtues in his book *The Road to Character* (2015). A résumé virtue is a concept you list on your résumé that brings external success in a career or in life. The résumé virtue is based on ideas of who you know, what you do, what you achieve or build that can impress the world. It's about winning, building, and discovering.

A eulogy virtue is an idea of wanting to get recognition at your funeral. It's based on your desire to be and do good. The eulogy virtue may mean giving up worldly success and status for a higher purpose or cause.

From my early years, both virtues resonated with me. One side of me wanted to build a higher status and win competitions, where the other side of me wanted to serve others in need through sacrifice and humility.

This battle is a struggle to be self-sufficient, working to avoid pain and weakness by focusing on ambition and career. This is the side of me that wants to have high status and win victories. There is nothing wrong with winning in competition, but if this part of nature goes unchecked or unbalanced from a deeper calling, the person can become a performer with no weight of character. David Brooks calls this "the shrewd animal."

This shrewd side of life addresses a deeper code of "an eye for an eye." You are what you earn, conquer, or achieve, and in return, you get what you earn. There are three major questions associated with this competitive voice inside of us:

How can I get ahead?

How does this work?

What will I achieve in status or success?

The other side of nature is more focused on internal caring. This side of me came in one important question: *Why did you make me?* How can my life make a difference? Who needs what I have to offer?

After a lot of pain in my teens, by my senior year, my outward image seemed better than it had ever been. Even in the yearbook, I was labeled the cutest and best dressed for senior year. The cheerleaders even picked me to be homecoming king! I had the positive nicknames in high school of "the Golden Boy" for having the lifeguard tan, "Hulky" for being muscular, "Speedy" for being able to run fast, and "Brother Taylor" because my grandfather was a minister. I liked every nickname. I wanted to feel special for something other than my stuttering. I had achieved some status for that brief time, but deep down I was still running to hide my struggles.

One struggle I remember was the quest to find a girlfriend who wanted to be serious with me and that I liked. I had quite a few dates and a few short romances, but I could not feel close to anyone.

There was one girl that seemed to like talking to me, and she was sought after by several popular guys. She dated a few of my friends. Her name was Tamra. She was a star on the basketball and volleyball team and a very confident person. She spoke to me differently than the rest of the students. She seemed to be able to understand the pain I felt inside of me.

I now think we both hid our pain by our outward performance in sports. Although, she was also ranked among the highest in our class academically. I suspect we both felt like misfits deep down and found relief in our mutual acceptance as we talked—at least I did.

Tamra shared some of her pain in life with me, like her relationship with her mom. I wanted nothing more than to be her "knight in shining armor." It felt that she touched me on a soul level. It was perhaps a case of a crush, but I still have good thoughts of her today.

I felt she could see the flawed person I was, and either identified with that or wanted me to be freed from my feeling of inferiority. She had a hold on my heart, so much so that after I graduated high school, I decided to leave the safety of my home and go to the college where she had gone a semester before. No one in my immediate family had ever been to college. So, I did it in the hope of winning her love.

This was a huge leap, and I don't think I would have made the jump without the hope of finding my true love. I followed Tamra to the University of Arkansas in Fayetteville, visiting the college one month before classes began. The hope I felt made me get on a little plane by myself, for first time and fly 180 miles away and leave everything I knew.

Many authorities in education testing said I would not make it in college after receiving an eleven on the ACT, but my focus was on proving myself and following the best voice of encouragement, the girl who saw through my mask to the real me. I can still feel the hope she gave me in my heart as I reflect on this now.

A big disappointment came to me when I found out that Tamra, who had gone to college a semester ahead of me, was transferring to another college as I was moving into the university dorm. I had to face the truth I feared: she was not romantically attracted to me. Still friends today, Tamra told me what she remembered the most about me was my honesty because it was unusual. I was more honest with her than anyone else because she was open with me in return and *saw* me. She was the first female I could be vulnerable with without any physical part to the friendship.

When she transferred, I felt I was all alone. I thought to myself, *How am I going to succeed in college? Why am I in college?*

As if Tamra leaving wasn't bad enough, the next thing I knew, all my classes were being cut. My tuition hadn't been paid on time from the State Rehab Grant, and all my classes were dropped. I lost it. I considered going back home. I cried as I sat on a bench thinking "I'm not cut out for college, and the girl I thought I loved does not love me." What was I going to do?

While I was on that bench, a man noticed me and asked me what was wrong. I told him all my classes were dropped, and I was unenrolled.

"Come with me," the man said.

He wore a pressed, navy blue suit and had a hard look on his face. I had no idea if he was going to put me back on the bus for home or take me to jail.

He took me to the enrollment office. It turned out he was Head Registrar for the University of Arkansas. He told the office to override the system and put me back into every class I had been removed from.

"Today is your day. You're reenrolled in all your classes," he said with a gracious smile.

I thanked him and then I don't remember seeing him ever again. I wondered how this important person, a stranger to me, noticed and why he decided to help me in this weak moment. Before this, I had been feeling like no one cared about me. Him helping me gave me a boost of hope that a greater force was watching over me, at least for that moment. The truth was I still felt alone in a strange new place.

In an attempt to find my voice in this new place, I again turned to sports. I became a walk-on football player in the spring of 1984 for the Arkansas Razorbacks. I wanted to prove to everyone I could be somebody. Even my dad was proud of me because he loved the Razorbacks. The Arkansas Razorbacks has the loyalty from the whole state of Arkansas. I thought in my heart if I could become an Arkansas Razorback football player then I could be somebody.

One of the first few days of my spring football practice, the team had to run through different training exercises. There was a transition from the Coach Lou Holtz to Coach Kenny Hatfield during this time. Each player had to call out their names before running through each drill. It came to my turn, and I couldn't say my name because of my stuttering. I could feel every man's eyes on me from the line forming behind me and the coaches in front of me. Their eyes were asking what was wrong with this guy. I could hear some players laughing behind me. One coach looked at the other assistant coaches and was confused as to why I couldn't say my name. After what felt like an eternity, I finally managed to say it. After that day, the coaches would say it for me as I approached the new drill.

"Chris Taylor, go!" On the bright side, at least they learned my name quickly.

I made the first cut of the football tryouts, but as time passed, I began to lose hope of ever playing in a real game. I eventually quit the football team. I weighed 165 pounds and was five feet seven inches. I was strong for my size. I could bench press around 335 pounds and could squat around 550 pounds. I could almost dunk a basketball and had a 4.5-second forty-yard dash. Yet, I felt I was not being noticed by the coaches for my athletic potential, which was average for the University of Arkansas.

I *was* noticed for another reason. I was in the training room a lot for relief from shin splint problems. The Head Razorback football trainer, Dean Webber, noticed my speech impediment. One day, he brought me into his office and told me he had a speech impediment as well. He recognized my struggles to speak, which wasn't how I wanted to be noticed. Webber's words of encouragement meant a lot to me. Again, I was noticed for a struggle I had, and not for what I was trying to be noticed for. After a few months, I still walked off the team with little hope I would ever be noticed by anyone other than in the training room which helped people with injuries. I think I had finally surrendered my hope of sports giving me an outlet to be seen. With that last ditch effort of hope lost, I was very down. The identity voice of "Why am I here?" became louder in my head.

A few days later, I thought of why I'd even left home to begin with. I had no idea who I was. I'd lost hope. I felt embarrassed. How would I tell my dad I quit the football team?

I felt completely alone. I remembered that six months earlier, people called me by my many positive nicknames. But now all of that seemed lost.

I was losing all that I had built up before graduating in my senior year of high school. It seemed as if the roles and performances I played were a shadow of who I really was. The feeling of not being adequate was coming back from my middle teens, only this time I had no one to talk to about it. Every day seemed like a blur after I quit in football. I felt empty with no purpose, hope, or identity. Who was I to the world? I could not survive. Feelings of loneliness and depression felt like drowning in the sea. The darkness became greater than I had known in the past. I felt that only my mom could love a loser like me. I did not want my family back home to worry about me, so I bottled it up. I thought everyone loved the mask I had developed to hide my shame.

I was like an actor with no more roles to play. I remember a very dark moment. I was alone in my dorm room. I had desperate, crazy thoughts of killing myself. I considered ways to take my life. At one point, I gathered a rope and brought it to my dorm room. I had nothing and no one to turn to. My image I'd depended on for my identity was gone. With everything I'd been trying to achieve, I felt I failed.

I feared my dad was right. *I would never amount to anything.* I felt I was a loser.

I was looking for a reason to live in this dark hour.

This was the first time I saw myself without the mask I had worked so hard to build. For years, I tried to prove my worth to others and hide my pain and insecurity with another identity. I had hit bottom.

Trusting in my strengths and hiding my weakness was no longer working. I believed I was a failure who no one seemed to care about, except maybe my mom. Loneliness is a part of many people's lives, and often the fear of abandonment and failure takes over during our darkest moments. It was in these instances I normally ran and hid by numbing the shame with alcohol, but this time, I considered the alternative: death.

Fearing the prospect of ending my life, I was in no hurry. My emotions were getting darker. I remember leaving my dorm to go to our restroom in the hall. While in there, a fellow student who lived on my hall came in and he spoke to me. Maybe he noticed I looked down or depressed. He asked if I would like to join him and a group of friends for a Bible study.

Although I'd grown up in a church, I believed that anyone who spoke about God, Jesus, or the Bible on any day other than Sunday was a religious "Jesus Freak." But I was searching to belong somewhere, and I believed I had no other place to go. So, I accepted the invitation, maybe out of desperation.

These guys weren't part of my perception of the cool crowd who drank and played sports; they were more studious. At first, I felt they were more the nerdy type, but they seemed to genuinely care about me. The ringleader of the group was Jim McConnon. He seemed older than most of us on the dorm floor. Turns out he was an officer in the US Army who came back to attend law school. He seemed to live with purpose and focus. Others in the study that night were a quiet pre-med student, an engineering major, a gamer, and another college freshman like me.

That night, during Bible study, the question I had been asking internally for many years arose. "Why did God make me?" The answer was found in Isaiah 43:7:

"Everyone who is called by my name, whom I created for my glory, whom I formed and made."

That verse relieved me. I'd been created for a purpose! Isaiah 43:7 made me feel significant. A light had turned on and I began to see my life had meaning and purpose.

According to researcher William Damon (2008), one's purpose is a question that many people, young and old, wres-tle with. It was true of me as a nineteen-year-old and it still rings true of me now as a fifty-six -year-old. We need mean-ing to our existence.

I found out early in life, I was made to bring glory to God, and even now I am still learning to continually look deeper into what that means. It was clear early on that bringing glory to me or proving myself had failed to deliver satisfaction on its own. For me it was my faith that helped me to find a purpose bigger than myself. My saving thoughts were that if God made me for His glory, surely, He made my stut-tering mouth as well.

I realized the struggle was bigger than just me. This was the hope I had been searching for in my long-time question I asked behind my childhood home.

Why did You make me?

This new insight led me down the road that sparked my purpose. So, how could I fulfill my purpose when it was still unclear? How could my stuttering serve my ultimate purpose?

The shame of not measuring up and fearing no one would love me because I was a failure almost took my life.

Researcher, author, and speaker Brené Brown describes shame as "the intensely painful feeling or experience of believing that we are flawed and therefore unworthy of love and belonging—something we've experienced, done, or failed to do makes us unworthy of connection. I don't believe shame is helpful or productive."

It was a steady but slow journey to embrace the part of me I believed was a shameful weakness. I tried to find strength in my life for so long. Looking at my strengths and the location of my pain was a good place to decide on a purpose for my life. Until that moment, I'd only seen my weakness as a liability threatening to destroy me.

In 2016, I got a hint of shame forming in my then fourteen-year-old son, Zachary. He had an incident where he and a few friends ventured outside from the YMCA to a gas station. A man, who seemed drunk, drove up and tried to tell the boys to get in the back of his truck. After a few moments of feeling threatened, Zachary decided to slip away and report this to the police while the other boys argued with the man.

A few days later, Zachary quietly mentioned his doubt in running. He felt if he had been stronger, he wouldn't have run. The officer said kids had been abducted in the area. He later told the boys that getting away and reporting the man was the right thing to do.

I could relate to the same shame Zachary was going through—being afraid and running away. There was an internal voice that Zachary was hearing. It's a voice we all can hear during certain situations. *Am I brave and strong? Do I have what it takes? Am I popular? Am I attractive? Who am I?* The fear of being unworthy, or flawed, is a core part of our human condition.

The response to quit and hide your shame versus striving to achieve and excel comes from how you view your strengths and limitations. This was my first great hurdle, pushing me over the first major threshold of life. I had to believe what I viewed as my "weak flaw" was really helping me grow stronger.

Seeing our limitations, or weaknesses, as a source of strength is a much-needed view in our society. As I began to believe in my weakness, not as a liability but as an asset for my growth, I found my stuttering was also a place of impact and influence.

This is where University Research Professor Carol Dweck (2016) comes in. She discusses two mindsets in her work that she has seen in emerging young people, "growth mindset" and "fixed mindset." This theory shows how different people learn to view obstacles, challenges, effort, criticism, and successes of others. A person with a fixed mindset sees things like talent or intelligence as fixed. There is so much information with very little room for improvement. For example, if you score badly on a test, you might say, "I'm stupid" or "I'm not smart."

Dweck writes on the fixed mindset as:

I've seen so many people with this one consuming goal of proving themselves—in the classroom, in their careers, and in their relationships. Every situation calls for a confirmation of their intelligence, personality, or character. Every situation is evaluated: Will I succeed or fail? Will I look smart or dumb? Will I be accepted or rejected? Will I feel like a winner or a loser? (p. 6)

Conversely, with the growth mindset, there is always hope for improvement. If you do badly on a test and have a growth mindset, you might say, "I did not study hard enough" or "I have to work harder." If you miss a tackle in the football game, you might say, "I have to improve my focus or technique on the next play."

On the growth mindset, Dweck (2016) writes: "In this mindset, the hand you're dealt is just the starting point for development. This growth mindset is based on the belief that your basic qualities are things you can cultivate through your efforts."

To cultivate the growth mindset in young people, she adds:

> Don't praise intelligence or talent, praise the work ethic … [We] can praise wisely, not praising intelligence or talent. That has failed. Don't do that anymore. But praising the process that kids engage in: their effort, their strategies, their focus, their perseverance, their improvement. This process of praise creates kids who are hardy and resilient.

As an educator myself, I will say our education system causes youth to become addicted to validation. Many teachers are unknowingly teaching an "all or nothing" mindset in young people, which is based on fear and survival. In the education system, youth are being told their scores on the ACT will impress leaders in higher education institutions—which isn't completely true. The true part is the weight of the money for scholarships mostly hinges on scores on the ACT.

I believe the growth mindset can improve the playing field in education. Personally, I'd rather have a student with a growth mentality believing they can improve their abilities rather than a person with a fixed mentality who believes they are limited only by what they know.

The struggle is to overcome labels that educators, and the world, put on others like smart versus average. I know making the Dean's List feels good, but is it useful in the long run? It might feel good now, but it doesn't answer the bigger question:

What is the purpose of one's life?

In this next chapter, you see the conflict that goes on inside of us between the competitive drive to win and the desire to hear noble words spoken about us at our funerals. The truth is, we all have weaknesses and vulnerabilities. To get to your true self it means to own what you feel strongly about as much as what you feel weak about. To own what you like about yourself and to own what you dislike about yourself. You might find what you dislike or find embarrassing to be your greatest source of strength.

SECTION 2

Achiever Voice

CHAPTER 3

The "White Horse"

Purpose

On the road of vocation, we sometimes find ourselves needing to do the right things for the wrong reasons.

PARKER PALMER

Armed with a new purpose for my life, I started to gain popularity for my courage and ability to be bold even though I had a stutter. Mentors in my life began praising me for my willingness to share my story with people and how I seemed unafraid in the face of adversity.

I was still fearful of looking foolish, but my weakness had prepared me to work through my anxieties with sharing my journey of faith—perhaps more than someone who had no problem talking. I believed I had greater courage in telling people about my faith because I learned every day how to overcome the shame of what I thought people thought and said about me. Facing my fear was possible because I saw a purpose in something bigger than me.

I felt my strength grow in the middle of my vulnerability. I acquired a gift of building relationships with people quickly through similar identity struggles. I wanted to make people feel comfortable being around me by acknowledging my stutter as a struggle I had. That seemed to at least disarm the fear I felt, and it was a step in being real with people. People respond better than we think they will when we can be real and vulnerable.

I started to feel like I was on a white horse. I was a man on a mission. I gained confidence and boldness. One of my newly discovered teachings in the Bible that lifted me was a story where the Apostle Paul, an author of several books in the new testament, prayed and asked God to take away a "thorn in his flesh, a messenger of Satan" and God responded by saying: "No, Paul! My grace is sufficient for you, for My power is made perfect in weakness" (2 Corinthians 12:9 [NIV]).

Follow my line of thinking here. This quote was proceeded by Paul explaining why he was given this thorn in the flesh. He said it was to keep him from becoming overly proud because he had been given so many gifts. Part of the way I learned to grow and survive was to construct stories for myself. My faith grew while hearing tales like the Apostle Paul. Learning his story helped me to construct better stories for my life and challenges without being depressed over my speech impediment "thorn in the flesh." The power of my belief was God allowing me to struggle with stuttering to strengthen me for the tasks I had ahead of me, my greater purpose.

An event that helped my faith prosper was in 1987, when I finished my undergraduate studies at the University of Arkansas in Fayetteville. I was asked by my spiritual mentor, to join a ministry he had started. My mentor asked me to go to another university in rural Monticello, Arkansas, to start a campus ministry. Monticello was five hours from Fayetteville and two hours from Hot Springs, my hometown. This was my second big transition, and being alone on a journey, I accepted because I felt this was a challenge, and I wanted to prove I was the man. It felt like I was a part of a mission in special forces to be asked to do this. I was on a "white horse."

It was scary to leave the nest in Fayetteville and go out on my own, but this time, I knew I had a mission, and I was prepared to be challenged. In fact, I liked the challenge of embarking alone. But to be honest, it was depressing at first. I had to go and make new friends and a new life.

When I first got there, my mentor went with me to help me meet a few people on the campus. One of the groups we first connected with was the football team. We met with Head Coach Tommy Barns. He told my mentor and I that I could meet players by helping out during practice. He also, soon after, allowed me to be the water boy and travel with the team to games. I very much needed my mentor/boss to be with me to help me in the initial stages of this ministry at a new school to have courage.

One memorable day during practice, I followed one of the assistant coaches, Coach P, onto the field as he spoke to part of the team. He was known to be a challenging person. When he saw me, he mocked my stuttering with facial contortions in front of the players. I was instantly brought back to feelings of shame and feeling small. He embarrassed me in front of sixty players, while they laughed.

After practice, I went home, believing the whole team thought I was some kind of a freak. No one was going to want to associate with me. I feared they would make fun of me too.

That night at my house alone, I prayed, "Lord, I am not sure what everyone will think about me now. I came here to connect with these players, and I was made a laughingstock."

The next day, I went back to campus, hoping the players would still talk to me and not be ashamed of my presence. Then, a miracle happened.

I sheepishly went by some of the football players' dorms and one of the players saw me said something that changed my life.

"You are one of us now."

"What do you mean?" I asked.

"Coach P picks on all of the players he likes," he said.

I was shocked as I listened to his disclosure. Coach P calling me "zero" or "dumb as wood" meant he liked me and wanted me to get better. I was so overwhelmed with relief and joy that I went to the restroom and took a moment to breathe a sigh of relief.

To my amazement, the pain and humiliation helped me be more accepted by the team. The coach's mocking was a tool that opened the hearts of others, including my own. I was truly becoming a part of the team. I needed to experience this humiliation while on my "white horse" so as not to grow a pride that was based only on me. I got a glimpse of God at work which took the pressure off me having to maintain an image of myself that makes people prideful.

The "white horse" of my ego needed experiences, like with coach P, to cross the bridge between my ego-driven white horse and my true self which was an instrument in God's hands with "power made perfect in my weakness."

Coach P mocking me was a sobering reminder that the power of the white horse I was riding to save people needed humility to make the greatest impact. At that point, I wasn't ready to truly embrace the side of me that was immensely defined by my limitation. After the experience of humiliation, I realized Coach P's ribbing actually helped me connect with players on the team in spite of the pain it caused. I do not recommend that as a way to help stutterers, but my faith helped me to see what I could not see at first. God allowed me to suffer to help me not to be prideful, and it helped the team feel like I was one of them.

At the beginning of this chapter, I mentioned the quote by Parker Palmer regarding doing the right thing for the wrong reason. This is like saying no truly moral climb of a mountain can last if one's only purpose is reaching the top. The white horse image can't endure rough weather if you are the object of your worship and the savior. Ultimately, I was made to worship something greater than myself. The white horse is good, but without honestly confronting yourself and your vulnerabilities, you can become arrogant and not humble.

My natural way to protect myself was to build an image to hide behind, like the white horse. According to psychologist Carl Jung, horses symbolize instincts and primal drives of human beings. My drive to protect myself was to have the appearance of success and competence in my social groups.

In a sense, the white horse was still a good symbol of me trying to save myself while doing the right thing. The confident, ego-protecting white horse I am talking about is helpful in giving young people the confidence they need in the early stages of life. I frequently say my sons are "often wrong, but never in doubt." But if a young person only has confidence and has not surrendered to humility, this could lead to a life of self destructive arrogance.

It wasn't until Coach P exposed my insecurity that I first started to realize I had been riding in the direction of insecurity and pride motivated by my fear of failure. My desire started to grow to free myself from the weight of fear I was carrying from the unhealthy insecure pride I had developed while riding the white horse. To more fully embrace my calling to love others as I loved myself, I needed growth that could only come through some little deaths in my false white horse image. The realization was that my true weakness was not stuttering but arrogance and self-reliance. I was beginning to gain a glimpse of a humbler focus on the better path through God's glory and my suffering.

In spite of my humbling moments, I was still on the white horse running partially on the approval of mentors in my life. Despite being on the white horse, I deep down knew my ministry success was Christ's work through me, but I was still heavily relying on me and my own strength. The miracle I saw was several student leaders on that campus becoming Christians and joining our group. Their support helped reach other students on the campus. During the first nine months, heads of a fraternity—Dennis, Rodney, Joey, Ray—and leaders on the football team—Jeff, Anthony, Brad, and Brian—all came to a deeper faith in Christ. We eventually grew to have 120 to 150 students attending our weekly meetings. It was a real movement.

The more I began to accept my purpose, to reach people through God's love, the more confidence I gained in myself and my ability. Confidence is important in all aspects of life, including sports, business, school, and the early development of a healthy ego, which is the part of our self that absorbs praise rather than feelings of defeat.

This is the helpful side of the white horse ego: confidence and resilient hope during challenges and setbacks. If we find our white horse in a purposeful mission, it helps us in the thrill of victory and the agony of defeat. We feel linked to something bigger than ourselves.

Many young people are often known to have this white horse confidence that always finds hope within struggles. This is an important trait for our young people when we send them into the world. Their white horse helps them become resilient and live in an optimistic mindset as they share their noble mission in ways like in setting people free from an oppressive government, from spiritual meaninglessness, or from deadly cancer.

Like most good things, success and struggle can cause pain if the ego becomes inflated with arrogant pride and self-reliance. It's a double-edged sword. On one side, the heroic white horse can be useful for survival and hope, but on the other hand, a focus on praise from the crowd or mentors can cause us to forget the humble places we came from in the fight to set people free. Arrogant self-reliance has caused many great leaders to have great falls.

I have recently heard a quote that the ego is the anesthesia for stupidity. The ego is tricky in that it can turn good things into a means of pride and self-centeredness by taking the focus off of the mission. The danger is that a once small ego can be inflamed, thus creating a larger ego filled with narcissist tendencies. The challenge is not to let success go to the head and to embrace humility over arrogance. Everything can become a substitute for, or subtle distraction from, purely altruistic motives. For example, when you tell a secret at a party, you may misplace the love of popularity over love of friendship.

I loved the praise and applause that came with acknowledging my ability to be bold and overcome adversity. There is nothing wrong with these adorations until you realize you need them, causing your mindset to shift the focus to yourself. Success can become an addiction, numbing the deeper pain of life. The image we have created in the eyes of others can become exhausting to maintain.

The white horse can be a good thing until it becomes a persona to maintain and be praised for. The ego is sometimes pictured negatively, yet a young person can still benefit from the feeling of being protected by a naive persona, of having an invincible force. Like an acorn, the fragile seed inside is protected by a hard outer shell before it builds roots. The white horse operates as a protective outer shell for your soul. But the shell can rot the seed if it does not come off soon enough.

David Brooks has identified two mountains in his book, *The Second Mountain* (2019). In the book, he describes much that I can relate to on my journey. He relays some important parts to the journey like the "Instagram Life," the "Insecure Overachiever," "The Valley," and "The Wilderness." All necessary parts in moving from the first mountain of life to the second mountain. For me, I can see my Instagram life as when I was winning over the campus and having success. I can see the valleys from my encounter with humiliation from Coach P and, as you will see, my failure with my mentor by being too focused on pleasing him.

We spend the first half of life climbing a mountain meant to challenge and set goals. We can feel invincible like a knight on a white horse. Nevertheless, we need small losses in life to get a glimpse of the second mountain. The next mountain becomes a place of surrender in order for a greater purpose to emerge within the world and its needs. If the world needs my ability, then I must surrender to suffering as part of my calling.

Early in life, we need the boost of a white horse to hold us up, give us hope and purpose to endure the ups and downs while climbing the mountain. Though the white horse is a symbol of positive growth, it isn't without its dangers. The white horse can become a "dark horse" driven by arrogant appetites and desires. The heroic white horse of human nature is always in danger of being pulled to the dark side through arrogance and self-sabotage.

The danger in the first part of life is trading our "passion for glory" which comes from a line in the song "The Eye of the Tiger" by Survivor (1982). The song was created for the movie *Rocky III*.

Risin' up, back on the street
Did my time, took my chances
Went the distance, now I'm back on my feet
Just a man and his will to survive

So many times, it happens too fast
You trade your passion for glory

Can you see the positive white horse in these lyrics with the words "the will to survive?" The song was a representation of focus, rising from the bottom of the ranks, and surviving no matter what was thrown in your path. The potential for the white horse to become the arrogant white horse can be seen in the words, "So many times it happens too fast. You trade your passion for glory."

I was a twenty-two-year-old, and I saw a movement on a college campus. The danger to my soul was the potential to believe I made it happen. It is hard not to let such early success go to your head. Early success in my life helped me to get on the white horse, but the valleys and wilderness that came later saved me from the cancer of arrogant pride. The more focused we are on our own glory the more dangerous it becomes to be on the white horse.

Is the persona you are living driven by the need for others' approval? As you grow into your true self, seeking too much approval will distract you from finding your authentic voice. We are trained early in life to seek approval from our parents, school, bosses, etc. There is nothing wrong with following directions, but you also must learn to listen to your own heart. Don't be ashamed of having a white horse that has helped you win many battles in the first half of life. I discovered that finding a humble white horse can be better than the arrogant white horse mission. We can do better in the race of life if we have confidence mixed with humility. To find this we need to understand our strengths as well as our weakness.

In the next chapter, I will outline the beginning of my journey to lose my mask which caused me to question my white horse persona for the first time. I had been living to please others, and I needed to begin the journey to set good boundaries with others.

CHAPTER 4

Letting Go of Your Loyal Soldier

Chapter 4

We must let go of the life we have planned so as to accept the one that is waiting for us.

JOSEPH CAMPBELL

Beginning a new journey can be difficult, especially when you are leaving the safety of your home as I did, but you don't always have to do it alone. It helps to have a guide or mentor to help you gain courage and find your purpose, which sometimes involves finding the white horse. Everyone needs a guide, or mentor, to help throughout life. Someone who sees a gift in them. Someone who says you are good. The term "mentor" dates back to Homer's eighth-century classic *The Odyssey*, one of the oldest works we have of Greek mythology. A mentor shares knowledge and wisdom with a less-experienced companion.

According to Anthropologist Joseph Campbell, a mentor is like a "Threshold Guardian" who tests the resolve of the mentee to continue the quest at hand. A mentor is like a guide to help the less experienced person leave home and fight the battles ahead. A mentor is an important person who knows how to guide youth to reach their greatest potential.

There have been many mentors in my past who have noticed me on the football field, in my vocation, and in other places in life. My mentor, previously mentioned in the last chapter, hired me out of college to go to a campus in southern Arkansas. My first two years of leading the campus there went great. I was getting a lot of applause on my performing white horse.

Something began to change inside of me in my third year. I had gotten married at the end of my second year of leading campus ministry. I married Faith Parkinson of Conyers, Georgia. Marrying Faith and having her join me as part of my journey caused me to become more aware of my own heart and desires. I started to feel more motivated to know who "Chris Taylor" truly was without performing. I became more aware of my desire to find my own voice apart from other people's voice. When we're young, we can give coaches, teachers, mentors in our life a sort of a hero status. It is harder to disagree with them when you're young and you want to feel valued and receive recognition. Our mentors often give us a hero status as well.

I have always believed my father, coach, and other mentors were all proud of me and loved me. I was especially valued for my willingness to take on the challenges and make the tackles. The problem was I got lost somewhere along the way in my desire to achieve and please. I could not separate my mentors' voices from my own.

Achievement and praise are important, but the soul longs for more. I desired to be understood for more than my achievement. I knew I had to perform in the world, but my soul, deep down, wished for love and authentic safe connections more than the status of my achievements.

One of my mentors really believed in me as the guy he once said he would "take to hell with a bucket of water." To me that meant he felt I was courageous. There came a time my mentor told me he "felt cut off from the head up," which I took to mean he felt only his head and not his heart. We men are often taught to shut down our hearts and emotions to push through to our missions. In a battle it can be useful to not get caught in your emotions; the problem is if we ignore our hearts too long, we can see life as impersonal and can disconnect our heads from our hearts.

In an interview with Peggy Orenstein (2020), author and researcher, she interviewed one hundred boys between the ages of sixteen and twenty-two. She talks about the core issue of boys as, "being cut off from their hearts."

Orenstein also said when she asked boys to give their impression of the ideal guy, they would list things like, "stoicism, sexual conquest, dominance, aggression—or this weird combination of being both aggressive and chill—athleticism, wealth." And they would talk about "training themselves not to feel or training themselves not to cry."

There came a time where I had to face my heart. It was the straw that finally broke the camel's back, revealing I had been carrying the weight of performance for too long. A former mentor and boss told me he had given the manager the *"power to fire me"* if I didn't do reports of my weekly performance. This was a reasonable request, but something stirred inside of me that day that I could not shake off.

I did not want to do the performance weekly log reports. Truthfully, I now know I was afraid the performance reports would show how I did not measure up to the image I thought others had of me or of what I had of myself. I was afraid I would never measure up even if I wrote the reports.

I began to feel, for the first time, I think, that I had been riding the heroic white horse to gain approval more than the importance of my mission. After my mentor who was my friend and boss told me he gave the manager power to fire me, I became depressed and unmotivated for months. It almost felt like I was grieving a loss.

Now I know I was beginning the process of losing the false image I developed because of my need for approval. I lost my sense of self during this important time in my life.

I was divided in many ways. I wanted to be the man my wife thought I was; instead, I felt deflated, without a clear view of my purpose.

My young mind thought, "If forgetting to turn in reports could get me fired, then what was the point of anything else? I felt the fear that after all I had done, I still wasn't measuring up." I was only twenty-eight years old, and I was having an identity crisis. I know now the crisis of identity was a necessary step in order to begin listening to my own voice. I felt something had to change, and I knew that meant I may have to leave the mentor that meant so much to me.

In a week or two, I called my mentor to set up a meeting. With anxiety lacing my body, I drove hours to meet with him and tell him in tears I had to take another path. Yes, I was crying, I believe. He did not seem to understand why I would resign, and I could not explain it very well. I desired to feel my heart and his in this meeting. I was trying to get his encouragement and blessing. This was my first step to listening to my own voice. Driving home I felt sadness and freedom at the same time.

Richard Rohr, in his book *Falling Upward* (2011) suggests that to move from the first half of life to the second, we must discharge our "loyal soldier." Perhaps this is the meaning of being a rider on a white horse having to take little steps to get off the white high horse like shedding the shell of an oak tree acorn so the seed can grow. The loyal soldier is the early voice that protects us during the first half of life. The loyal soldier focuses on early instruction, praise, and reprimand from the early authorities in life. The Loyal Soldier is the voices of all early authority figures (p. 46). The loyal soldier is the elder brother in Jesus' parable of the prodigal son (Luke 15:25-32). The elder brother thought his loyalty entitled him and he saw his total goodness tied to his loyalty. What he did not realize was that his loyal goodness also kept him from the celebration of his brother and his true heart.

These voices are important in early life but can hinder us later. Commands like, "look before you cross the street," "don't do drugs," and even "do your staff reports" are all important statements that give much-needed structure early in life. We require discipline, accountability, and order for a healthy, emotional life, but we also need healthy boundaries to take responsibility and turn the other cheek. At the time,

I did not have healthy boundaries between me and those I needed approval from.

> *"When you discharge your Loyal Soldier, it will feel like a loss of faith or loss of self. But it is only the death of the False Self."*
>
> (ROHR, 2011, P. 50)

My loyal soldier was riding on a white horse, but it could not take me to the next level leading to my true self.

I owed a lot to my father and mentors, but my need for approval became unhealthy. I had the desire to find and express more of my own voice even though I still had no clue what it sounded like.

Identity theorists such as Erik Erikson, a developmental stage theorist, and James Marcia (1960), a child development theorist, suggest the stronger identities have had a crisis (conflict) or exploration period. This means that a crisis is good to form a healthy identity. This meant my children may come to disagree with me, but that is a form of becoming more whole as a person. My decision to go my separate way from my mentor was the first time I made a commitment apart from the approval of authorities in my life. The important thing about making a break from my mentors was that it was my choice ultimately, and I needed to make it. Today I still love my great mentor. We have a healthy relationship and are each doing the work God has called us to.

The big death blow to my false self came 20 years later when I was in my late 40's. This death brought with it a feeling of betrayal and it came without warning, or at least any warning I could recognize. This event involved someone separating from me. It took me all the way down. I now call it my necessary falling.

It has taken me a while to understand this experience as a necessary "death blow" to my prideful self. My pride set me up for a hard lesson. This part of my story occurred with people I trusted, who chose to separate from me and from an idea I had been developing. I know now this experience felt like a betrayal.

I want to say it is not my intention to judge anyone in this story. This is just my story and my experience, of which I am very grateful for now. I am sure there is completely another version of this story inside of the people with whom it took place. I decided not to share the details of this story, not wanting to harm anyone. I just want to say it was very painful and sent me into a depression.

In one swoop I felt like I lost my identity and a sense of self in my work. I felt lost and alone, not knowing who I could trust. This was humiliating. Were others willing to betray me? I did not know. I was fearful. At first, it was like being put in prison without knowing what I did wrong. I had received no warning about this separation despite some tensions I had with the guy who took the role of the leader.

As time went by, I grew more bitter and angry. I returned to a dark, place of shame and anger.

I felt humiliated.

Having trained as a counselor, I knew there was something missing. I could not shake this mental struggle. I went to a psychiatrist friend, Dr. Hall, who I worked under during an internship for my counseling master's degree. He asked me many questions before he made a diagnosis. He mainly knew I was anxious and depressed from my responses. I felt afraid and alone. I was worried about taking care of my family and what others my think about me. Dr. Hall said he thought I was experiencing betrayal trauma. Betrayal trauma can only develop from where I had once felt safety and security. "Betrayal trauma is *when the people or institutions on which a person depends for survival significantly violate that person's trust or well-being*" (Freyd 2008). I think this is what I experienced.

Dr. Hall told me I was shattered and needed to go walk by a river somewhere. Nature is a great healing place. The stream is a picture of a calm place. Trying too hard to understand what went wrong was sending me into greater darkness.

I needed to go and heal. I was questioning if I could ever trust again. The anger and shame I was feeling was a form of blaming myself for being used and betrayed. It was the feeling of being put in prison without being told what I did wrong. As a way to increase my current responsiveness, Dr. Hall gave me some depression and anxiety medication. I had all the symptoms of post-traumatic stress disorder (PTSD). I now realize I was having a funeral for my false self.

After months of feeling lost in the dark, I realized I had to take a harder look at myself. I had to ask myself what lead me into this. I doubted my ability to read people. For a while I felt like someone else unexpected will jump out and betray me again. I doubted who I could trust, my gifts, and even my life. I was cut off from my ability to trust others and myself. I was angry at being discarded and abandoned.

I needed to forgive both myself and those who involved me in this. Later, I went to a small group each week, I will call, The Edgar's Group, started by a man named Jay. He was a counselor, a mentor to me, and a friend. Every person in his counseling group seemed to be experiencing some type of loss, failure, or brokenness.

At first, I rejected the idea I needed this group of other struggling men. I didn't want to be part of a group where everyone talked about their deep-seated pain. It felt like, at first, I was in the loser's group and I did not want to be in the

58

category of a looser. I did not want to feel like that, but I now know I needed it because I had tried to hide behind a mask of being a winner for too long. I needed to surrender to the brokenness if I wanted to get a glimpse of my authentic self and a true since of God's love for me.

After a while of building trust, I found that part of the gift I gave to the group was being vulnerable in talking about my confusion and darkness. Jay Lloyd, the founder of the small group, understood me at a deeper level, looking past my performance. Jay had known me for a good while even while I was riding high on a prideful white horse. He had experienced my ego pride in the past. In this group my trust level grew. After a while, Jay told me my gift was to help men find their hearts while being honest about my own heart. I was cultivating a vulnerability in myself that allowed other people to experience and identify with my pain and weakness as well as find their own. Jay told me my greatest gift to the world was not performing on stage, but it was when I was in my heart and vulnerable.

Another form of healing came from the voice of a man named Bill Windle, who also helped me through this time of shame and darkness. Bill had been part of my early days of starting a new ministry to help people find their career calling. We met in 1998. A friend connected us and told me I could help Bill with his thoughts about his speech impediment.

Bill was the owner of a midsize construction company in Birmingham, Alabama.

As a friend of the family, Bill also knew my son, Will, who told Bill I was struggling. When Bill called me to meet, I accepted because I was still paralyzed by shame. The shame was around the fact I had let someone beat me in the game of life and leave me feeling all alone. I had the feeling like being hit and injured on the football field, and no one would come to pick me up. I was unsure anyone cared about me. When Bill and I met at a coffee shop, Bill said many things and asked me many questions but the one thing I remembered was he said, "We need you back on the field, not sitting on the sidelines. Other men need the Chris Taylor I know, the one that connected his heart to me and my sons. That Chris Taylor was fearless."

I told Bill I wanted to meet that Chris Taylor again someday.

Bill reminded me of who I was by making me remember my worth. He lifted me by connecting with me on a spiritual level, sitting with me when I was in the dark and reminding me I was more than what I could accomplish. One of Bill's favorite quote is, "Jesus Christ did not come to make bad people good, but to make dead people alive." Bill was a catalyst that brought me back to my true self.

Thanks to God's love through guys like Bill and Jay, I started to heal on a deeper level that day. If you want to help people come alive and find their voice, you must help them clarify their story. You have to sit with them in their darkness as they try to sort things out. You have to see something deeper than the surface-level mask and status that they have hid behind. You have to help them come alive and see their value in their soul.

Once I saw that my biggest battle was in my own heart; I could no longer believe that each defeat I'd gone through was someone else's fault. It was my own selfish desires and ego that lead me to these painful but necessary places. By breaking down my story, I began to see my own voice.

Something in us must die; otherwise, we won't be able to recognize a voice greater than the defensive, competitive desire to prove ourselves. This is the rite of passage to the second half of life. Few find this broken place and become grateful for it. I have seen many men unwilling to face their own brokenness just get smaller and continue to lay on the ground not coming alive.

Experiencing a feeling of betrayal in my 40's was the best medicine to help lessen my need for personal reassurance from every person I met. It also pointed me toward the few people who sat with me in the dark. They gave me the space to find my bearings and focus on a more powerful voice.

There's nothing more beneficial than a good dose of failure to help us dismount our white horse of self-confidence and self-reliance.

I know now that my surrender toward my true voice was underway during this time. Getting off the white horse is hard but necessary for a deeper identity. Truth be told, I gradually started to see my egotistical self-focus had made me unaware of other people's desires. I realized I'd taken people I cared about for granted and used them to meet my own needs. I'd been building a reputation, but the energy behind it was for recognition and approval. It took Bill, Jay and special groups to help me see how my white-horse ego had contributed to my own challenging experiences. I needed to begin to forgive both myself and those who I felt betrayed me.

I also found some relief in Parker Palmer's book called *Let Your Life Speak, (2000)* he said,

> *"We must withdraw the negative projections we make on people and situations—projections that serve mainly to mask our fears about ourselves—and acknowledge and embrace our limits and liabilities"*
> LET YOUR LIFE SPEAK (P.29).

My heart began to heal. Having friends help me battle for my heart allowed me to overcome my shame and insecurities.

The more I allowed myself to accept the dark place in my mind, without judgment or having people try to fix me, the more I began to see who I was truly meant to be. Men like Jay and Bill, who were also broken, showed me the power of God's love regardless of the performance.

If you sit in the dark with other broken people long enough, you will start to see the light. You learn to surrender your false self and begin a journey to a more authentic voice.

The lesson I learned, was that no one could destroy my soul unless I let them. I began to embrace the freedom. No one can take away from my soul anything unless I give it to them. I learned to forgive others when I accepted responsibility, which allowed me to embark on this new journey. I was able to let go of the image I created for myself and embrace the true meaning of being a child of God with a new family to fight with me. In the next chapter, I will discuss my path home and my resurrection toward my true self.

Maya Angelou stated in *Letters to My Younger Self,*

> *"You are only free when you realize you belong no place—you belong every place—no place at all. The price is high. The reward is great."*

Brené Brown interprets this in an interview with Lewis Howes (2017):

"I feel I belong everywhere I go, no matter where it is or who I'm with as long as I never betray myself. And the minute I become who you want me to be in order to fit in and make sure people like me is the moment I no longer belong anywhere."

The real effect of these relational challenges was for me to learn to own my part and forgive myself and others. I learned to forgive because I came to a humbler place of surrender. Now I cannot be knocked down as well because I do not have as far to fall. When we are on our noble white horse which some might call, a high horse, we have a farther distance to fall. But that falling can help us stand more solidly on the ground and find that true voice that is below the surface. It can open us up to seeing the author voice, which I begin to focus on in the next chapter.

SECTION 3

Author Voice

CHAPTER 5

Starting the Journey Home

Becoming Myself

It's taken time, many years and places;
I have been dissolved and shaken,
worn other people's faces...

MAY SARTON

The desire after great battles in life is often to come back home to where we first began our journey, so we can bring a cure to the world we discovered on our journey, which is commonly known as a final step in the "hero's journey." The hero's journey is a common narrative used in most movies that involves the hero who goes on an adventure, learns a lesson through challenges and adversity, wins a victory with newfound knowledge, then returns home transformed with the elixir. The victory I had to bring back to home was the victory over my own insecure ego.

The return home is in the desire to do things better or redeem the world. My personal journey involves becoming grateful for my pain and weakness, which had developed as a source of a more useful strength than the insecure drive to prove myself.

On my return home, I prepared myself by breaking the habit of running away to hide my insecurities behind a mask. I had two paths I could take: bitterness and anger, or joy and hope. My choice was which one I would surrender to. The real betrayal was me betraying myself, my own voice, by trying to be what others wanted me to be. This has not been a quick process. It took years fighting with my own ego to finally surrender to the greater peace I am now beginning to enjoy. My personal resurrection developed from dark nights of my soul. One of the steps to my resurrection after the death of my ego was to be connected to a community of broken men like myself.

My struggle made me different, but it also made me unique. If not for my stutter, I would have never learned how to open myself to my emotions. If not for my experience with leaving my first mentor, I would not have known my voice apart from seeking unhealthy approval. If not for the experience of betrayal and separation, I would not have connected to my deeper heart.

I found through fear I can be brave. Through pain, I can become strong. Through sadness, I can find joy. For every struggle, there was a lesson I learned. The greater lessons in suffering are meaningful if you are focused on something greater than yourself, and this comes through the death and resurrection of your inner being, which I call my true self made in the image of God. It was a reminder that my weakness and surrender was the path to true power. The way up or home is through the valley of the shadow of death.

Richard Rohr, in his book *Falling Upward (2011)*, states the desire to return home after early experiences come from two places. His idea points back to the desire for union found in the original connection with our mother and the possibility of a paradise where wrongs can be righted. Even those that come from a bad home have the seed of a possible and ideal paradise with the desire to right the wrongs (Pg88).

We each make sense of our world by attaching our experiences to a story. For example, after the attacks on September 11, 2001, people could only make sense of terrorism by placing it in a narrative about villains and heroes. Depending on their perspective, some people believed it was the result of America's abuse of power in the world. On the opposing side, some believed there were evil people in the world who hate Americans because of their rights and freedom.

Throughout history, the worldview of Christianity has had a profound impact on how many people operate in the world. The argument can be made that there were moments where the storyline made other people the problem, but when Christians allow the truth to set them free, they see the problem was from the core of their own selfish heart.

When we get it right, we begin to recognize our own heart is the real enemy once we've diverted our misguided attack. We see the sin in others as a result of the fall of Adam and Eve who chose to disobey God by eating the forbidden fruit. We see that evil pursues us in the world.

We are always fighting some type of enemy. An enemy can come in the form of a jealous friend, a spiteful coworker, or even fear within our own hearts. Enemies aren't just people we interact with. They can also be disguised as struggles within our own mind, causing us to doubt everything we say and do. The following statement can be found in the Bible, which reminded me of the real enemy:

"What causes fights and quarrels among you? Don't they come from your desires that battle within you?" (James 4:1 [NIV]).

The road home is about coming alive in our second half of life. One example of coming alive in brokenness would be the story of the jazz musician John Coltrane found in the book *Every Good Endeavor* (Keller, 2012). Even the title of the book comes from John Coltrane's intro to his album "A Love Supreme." I'd never listened to John Coltrane, but I can connect to his journey. The experience of Grace breeds creativity in people and gives meaning to life, love and work. Coltrane was a man driven by an external motivation and was later transformed through his internal motivation of God's love and grace. Just like Van Gogh, Picasso, and Monet loved painting, Coltrane loved his music. He struggled with an addiction to heroin and alcohol, like many other artists, which ultimately destroys later success. The difference for John was his spiritual experience, inspiring his work on a deeper, more personal level. He became more internally motivated by a supreme love based on his newfound relationship with God. In tribute to his new love, he wrote one of his greatest albums called *A Love Supreme*, where he shares his personal journey:

> During the year 1957, I experienced, by the grace of God, a spiritual awakening which was to lead me to a richer, fuller, more productive life. At that time, in gratitude, I humbly asked to be given the means and privilege to make others happy through music. I feel this has been granted through His grace. ALL PRAISE TO GOD.

This album is a humble offering to Him…May He help strengthen all men in every good endeavor.

John Coltrane found a deeper story in himself. He found an infinite love from a supreme power. He found his voice through seeing a bigger story that took his music to a higher level. His struggle with addiction brought him to a dark place where he was lost in his weakness and struggled to perform. But from that dark place, he was resurrected, finding humility and brokenness as a path to deeper worship with a new voice.

You might say that all of us are similar to John Coltrane as we struggle to come alive and return home to our true selves. A story lives in each of us, but we need to have the courage to find the love within and outside of ourselves to create a fresh voice.

Coltrane found the greatest motivation of all. He found a supreme relationship with God through love that not only transformed him but also saved him from an empty purpose. He claimed he found his true self through God and His Glory.

You can reflect on how your journey began, what battles you have fought, and hopefully, through this process, you can begin to uncover your true voice and find the hero's purpose inside. We need to learn to tell the story of our lives. There is a reason I want to help people find their voice in life. It comes from a story with no voice.

In a hero's journey, there is often a resurrection right after the darkest experience. Only through death can a hero be reborn, and this rebirth comes through suffering great tests. The path for the hero can have moments of the peace in the green pastures, and moments of war were you battle for your life. We each suffer and find relief in our own time and way. The early suffering has been linked to internal motiva-tion as we examine our story.

In a journal article interview titled Career Counseling and Family Therapy (2016), Mark Savickas, a well-respected theorist in career counseling and development said, "We actively master what we passively suffer." In an interview in 2012, Savickas was asked what the statement meant.] He had this to say:

> It's the most important thing I know. I believe each of us, early in life, in our family, there's something painful. What we do in life is to try to heal that hole in our hearts. So, if what upset us in the beginning is fear; the resolution, or strength, that person must develop is courage and bravery. We go from the passive suffering of fear to the active mastery of bravery. I'm looking for the pain. And, then work. Career counseling is about how you are going to use work to heal yourself.

We need to return home with a remedy for the sickness of the world that we grew up in. That sickness can be a lack of meaning or purpose to life's struggle. This sickness is what has left a burden or hole in our hearts, in our journey, through the early part of life. That sickness may be fear or shame. That sickness can be a physical challenge or the cancer that killed my father. In our deepest vocational calling or voice, we need to tell the story so we can find our author inside to cure the problem we have encountered in the world. For instance, I want to see both young and older people find their calling and not just have a job or a career. For most, they will focus only on a job and career, but for those becoming aware of their deeper story, they have a chance of finding the deeper calling of their life.

Many have stated that the way to God is through humility.

Parker Palmer in his book *Let Your Life Speak* (2000) helps us understand humility as "where we are brought low, rendered powerless, stripped of pretenses and defenses, and left feeling fraudulent, empty, and useless." (P. 70)

In his book *Falling Upward* (2011), Richard Rohr attempted to define the inward journey during the second half of life.

> "I have prayed for years for one good humiliation a day, and then, I must watch my reaction to it. I have no other way of spotting both my denied shadow self and my idealized persona." (p. 128).

An example of a person who did not come fully alive on his journey home was my dad. I mentioned in the first chapter that part of my reason for writing this book was to go back and metaphorically save my father. My father was an example of a hero who helped everyone; however, it can become a curse when the belief in the well-being of others rests totally upon the hero's shoulders. My dad tried to carry responsibility for everyone, especially his children and extended family. Dad needed to let us fall off the bike and carry our own weight, though. Telling part of my dad's story has been a way to understand my own.

My dad died at the age of sixty-three from cancer. Dad had told my younger brother, Phillip, before he died to "carry everyone you can." Phillip had spent more time around my dad by working with him at our family hardware store. I believe "carry everyone you can" was the way my dad lived. It is a heavy weight I now feel I passed unintentionally to my children. I do not want them to suffer and struggle too much. I want them to have it easier than I did. Even though I know now the strug-gle is good, it is hard to fully accept that in my heart.

My dad, like me, may have tried to be god for his family. We certainly benefited from his protection, but I also believe the pain of life got to him because he could not see his story as well when he was living through it. I believe evil pursued my dad like it pursues me. The best door for evil to pursue me is through my desire to be responsible for what only God is responsible for. It is the desire to control others and life that opens the door for evil. There are many pains I cannot protect my children from in life. That is why I pray for them. But that does not erase wanting to pick them up when they are stressed or hurting.

Some of the tests my dad faced would be a challenge for any man, including Superman. When Dad was forty-nine years old, his first-born grandson, Alex, had a lot of complications at birth. Born premature, Alex weighed one and a half pounds and was in the hospital for nine months at a location one hour away from our family. Alex later developed cerebral palsy from meningitis, an infection in the spinal fluid. Alex is now thirty-three and has never walked. My brother and his wife, since they were eighteen years old, have had Alex to care for as well as raising two other children. They had to grow up real fast with this responsibility. Cleaning Alex and feeding him every day for thirty-three years. I know, being my father's son, that my dad also carried a burden for both Alex and my brother and his wife. I know my dad begged God to save Alex's life. God did save him, but he would never walk and would always need to have someone take care of him. I am sure my dad was also carrying the memory of pain that he and mom went through having their first-born daughter, my older sister, Kimberly, born dead. Kimberly weighed ten pounds, and I have seen pictures of her in a casket.

I know Dad carried these weights. Life can just knock the hell out of you at times. For the record, Alex has been one of the greatest blessings in our family, but that challenge was one in a long line my dad carried with his family. God knew our family would be blessed by Alex. My brother and I often say to each other now that when we get to heaven, Alex will be driving the bus with a beaming grin on his face that will make everyone else smile.

When my dad was in his fifties, I saw him sink lower emotionally. From the age of fifty-five to sixty, dad witnessed his best friend, his father, and his mother die within a span of five years. He seemed to lose some of the spring in his step. He seemed to drift a little bit. He had always been a strong person, able to do anything he set his mind to. I saw him turn to alcohol to deal with the pain. I have been tempted like that as well.

My hunch was Dad did not know how to find meaning in the losses he faced in his life. I do not believe he knew how to interpret his journey, and that also contributed to losing sight of purpose in this life and beyond this life. After facing so many tests, he was on a downhill slope. He seemed to get worn out in life.

At the age of sixty-two, he got cancer. I cannot help but believe his experience with despairs, weights in life, and losses caused his body to be more susceptible to the cancer. Smoking did not help either. Some of his last words reveal the weight he carried: "I am not afraid of dying. I just do not want to leave all of you." Dad made his family his focus and responsibility in life.

I think he worried we would have a hard time surviving without him. I think we all worried about that at first, too, including my mom.

I wish I could go back and have a talk with my dad. I would tell him what my son told me, "Dad, you have to let us go." I wish I could cheer him up as he often cheered me up. He was a cheerleader for me and, I think, most of my family including my uncles and cousins. He did not always know how to talk about his feelings and pains. He never complained to us because that would be a burden to us, and he had to carry that himself.

I have felt the same danger of midlife drifting, where my sadness is felt much more than joy. I have worried I could not be there enough for my children; I have been in danger of the same fate as my father. Watching the tests and pains my children face has been my hardest fight of faith thus far. Sometimes it feels unbearable for me, and I find relief even now in telling the story of how God has turned my pains into joy, my losses into hope and as I head toward home where all things will be made right.

CHAPTER 6

Stay on the Bus

Endurance

Many of life's failures are people who did not realize how close they were to success when they gave up.

Thomas Edison

The most challenging point of this journey to your authentic self is to not lose heart. While writing this book, I feared I wouldn't have anything original to say. The fear of failure made me want to quit and turn back. Many people have given up the moment they're close to success. There weren't many people I could talk to about writing, and there were times I wasn't sure how to be in the present moment without the fear of future failure.

I think much of our unhappiness comes when we're living in regret of the past or worrying about the future. Obsessing over previous regrets and future worries can take us away from our true self. One verse from the NIV Bible that has helped me is from the words of Jesus:

"Therefore, do not worry about tomorrow, for 'tomorrow' will worry about itself. Each day has enough trouble of its own"
(Matthew 6:34 [NIV]).

This verse does not say, don't plan for the future, but it says, do not worry about the future. When I worry about the future I cannot rest in the present. When I write and fret too much about if my writing will matter, then I lose my ability to be present with my soul. When I worry about saying my name if called on in a crowd, then I will have trouble saying my name. Most worry is about dwelling on things we cannot control.

Living in the present is a discipline that can be a challenge to achieve, but necessary for contentment, joy, and creativity. This may sound corny, but I finally redefined the meaning of success—not from what I could accomplish, but from what is inside of me that is gift to the world. I couldn't define success while ignoring what my soul seeks to be. My soul is a sacred place that desires authenticity over falseness and wholeness over division. For a while, I could run on achievement, but the yearning for more kept reminding me I still wasn't whole. Parker Palmer in his book, *Let Your Life Speak* (2000), described the soul as:

> The human soul doesn't want to be fixed, it simply wants to be seen and heard. The soul is like a wild animal—tough, resilient and shy. When we go crashing through the woods shouting for it to come out so we can help it, the soul will stay in hiding. But if we are willing to sit quietly and wait for a while, the soul may show itself. (p. 7)

My soul has rejected using superficial things to define myself by winning, accumulating, controlling, and seeking security. In my journey home, after my encounters with mentors, betrayal, and my false self, I came the closest to my true self soul in the wilderness. Like in the hero's journey, the times of testing forced me into a necessary wilderness for my soul to realize I had tried to be someone other than what God created me to be. Strength often comes from brokenness in a wilderness or desert experience. In the wilderness one faces thirst, lostness, sadness, aloneness, failure, and defeat. This is where one must face the earlier fears of life, which was for me, that I would never be anything. In the wilderness a person can gain intimacy with the true self if we do not die in the battle from the shame of not being enough.

In this wilderness of testing, I concluded I couldn't manufacture the success I thrived on in my earlier days. To acquire a connection with my soulful self, I had to endure and not focus on success as often defined by the world. People do not need another photoshopped flawless image, but they need the reality of an authentically flawed person seeking to grow and make progress.

I came to realize I needed to view my success more like a Major League batter in baseball. In Major League Baseball, a *good* hitter can average 275 hits per 1,000 attempts at bat. A player is considered a *great* hitter if his average is 300 hits per 1,000 bats. In other words, a player must endure the struggle and have the right mindset to stay optimistic for a hopeful future.

You must "walk by faith and not by sight" (2 Corinthians 5:7 [NIV]). Simply put, when you're in the wilderness and the path may be unclear, you must relax in the present and believe you will make it back home.

When I lost my way, I needed to be reminded of who I was. My faith helped me by telling me I was a child of God and that I was deeply loved. The realization was easiest to see when I wasn't consumed by the next achievement, because in the desert, achievements and trophies do not matter as much as food for the body and soul.

When I lost heart on this journey, I became short-sighted as I feared for my survival and the survival of those closest to me. In Jim Collins' book *Good to Great* (2001), he mentions the Stockdale Paradox. The lesson is from Admiral Jim Stockdale's eight-year experience as the highest-ranking United States military officer in the "Hanoi Hilton" prisoner of war camp during the height of the Vietnam War, where he was tortured twenty times. His paradox principle was that he never lost faith and found a way to make it home. He claimed those who didn't make it out of the camp were the optimists. Normally, this wouldn't be a bad thing, but in this case, the optimists lost hope in their anticipation of getting released by a certain date. They died of a broken heart, but Stockdale shared a great principle regarding the endurance of suffering and the process supporting the journey to true self. What was Stockdale's secret to survival? He said, "I never lost faith in the end of the story." Stockdale further said, "You must never confuse faith that you will prevail in the end—which you can never afford to lose—with the discipline to confront the most brutal facts of your current reality, whatever they may be" (2001, p. 85-86)

There is an endurance, or "walk by faith" phase, in this journey to our authentic voice. Just like Stockdale thought, "you must believe you will prevail." Finding your voice requires you to endure a walk of faith, which is similar to developing your work, art, or writing. You're going to strike out a few times, but it doesn't mean you have to quit. Believe in the end of the story not as an optimist of events but as a hopeful survivor.

In June of 2004, Arno Rafael Minkkinen stepped up to the microphone at the New England School of Photography to deliver the commencement speech. The speech has been titled "The Helsinki Bus Station Theory: Finding Your Own Vision in Photography." The speech was meant to show the listeners how to develop their art by enduring the early stages of the creative process. Minkkinen focused on the difference between success and failure, describing the creative process of life as different platforms on a bus station in Helsinki as a year in the life of a photographer.

Minkkinen said in part of his speech:

Suppose you took three years of your creative work to the art show. Then during the art show, your work resembled someone else's, so you got in a cab and headed back to the bus station because you discovered your art wasn't as unique as you thought. So, after three more years, someone says, your work looks like someone else's. So, the temptation is to go back to the station and start over on a new bus. Stay on the f***ing bus. Eventually, you will see the difference in your art. After a while, the buses will all go different routes and so will your creative work. For a period, your work may resemble someone else's, but eventually you will grow into your uniqueness as long as you stay on the bus.

This story represents the need to endure in your voca-tional story, your art, and your creativity in order to find your own voice of expression to the world. At first your work may have some resemblance to others' work that have impacted you, but you must know your own true voice will eventually surface if you "stay on the bus."

Just like my stuttering and other trials, I had moments when I fell into a depression and found unhealthy coping mechanisms that also hurt myself and those I loved. I tried to cope with the prospect I have nothing original to say. Truth be told, every idea is built on other ideas. However, the more I recognized the light of my purpose during adversity, the more I could recreate a better story in a more positive transformational way. Stories need to find a positive purpose amid weakness, trials, and wins if we are to endure on the road to discover our own story.

The point is to remain persistent and continue to cultivate your unique voice without constantly turning back. It doesn't mean you should never scratch a project, but remember most creators' early work, their voice, resembles some of the people they've been inspired by. If you persist, the bus routes leaving the station will all eventually branch off in different directions to different destinations, similar to the routes you take during your first phase of life, giving you the chance to develop your creative work. This means that in order to create something unique, you need to "stay on the bus" toward your art's true voice. Don't give up on your dream. If you have a dream, you must continue to cultivate and develop it. It can be very hard to keep writing, building, working for others, and not seeing your own unique voice emerge, but it's there; you just have to find it behind all the noise.

To get to your true voice, you have to focus on the ultimate destination. How are you getting out of your prison? How will you survive the challenge? What makes you believe in identifying your ultimate purpose, your personal contribution to the world? Eventually you will hear your own voice more clearly if you "stay on the bus." It is the hero's journey that we must understand and remain focused on.

CHAPTER 7

The Hero's Journey

Grant, Lord, that I may know myself, that I may know Thee.
SAINT AUGUSTINE A.D. 400

To become your whole self, I have connected the word *author* to show awareness and narration of your own story, connecting your past, present, and future. This is considered an identity milestone where a person finds a sense of wholeness through how one interprets or tells their story. The author's type of self is a milestone of identity development, placing the past, present, and future self together in a story that can help one make sense of their purpose through their life experiences. As humans, we seek completeness by telling stories of who we were, who we are, and what we hope to be.

It is good to look back and ask people what they remember about you. You have to decide if they remember your true essence or your false mask. Recently, a guy who I helped spiritually named Bret called me and shared two memories he has of me. First, he shared the story of when he saw me in his fraternity meeting room while many men were sitting around listening to me. Bret said I had a pretty hard time talking but remembered thinking he could never have the courage to speak like me, especially if he had a stutter like that. He did not remember what I was saying, but he recalled the perception he had of me.

The second story he shared was similar. He came to hear me speak in front of a crowd at a nearby college. Hundreds of students were there. The next part was not in my memory, maybe because I repressed it. But Bret said I had a really hard time speaking that day. He said he thought to himself if he was struggling like that in front of a group, he would feel angry at God.

The main points I got from these stories was the impact I was trying to make on people through my ability to motivate, but people were being inspired by something at a deeper level. It is humbling to see what God was doing through me was deeper than the performance I was giving. It was my weakness and struggle that spoke deeper than the words.

It has been adversity and times in the valleys and deserts that have helped strip away the drive to prove myself. It has been stories like these that have helped me surrender to receiving instead of thinking I am the giver. I now find myself more grateful for every person I experienced conflict with—grateful for my losses and grateful for my stuttering. All those struggles or weaknesses have presented as a gift to me: the power of forgiveness, letting go, and surrender. If I had not been knocked off my high horse, I would not have taken time to reflect on the true meaning of my life. All adversity helps us to be released from the false narratives of the past.

Humility and forgiveness are the most positive results of a deeper journey—reminding myself that other people's actions didn't make me who I am. In my false self, I damaged my soul and others around me when I tried to be something I was not. I was always focused on the applause and the nobleness of my cause. It is this struggle between strength and weakness that makes it hard to understand the paradox of how strength comes from weakness. This quote represents the movement from youth to maturity: Wilhelm Stekel quoted in *Catcher in the Rye* (1951) "The mark of the immature man is that he wants to die nobly for a cause, while the mark of a mature man is that he wants to live humbly for one. (p. 188)

Now, part of my mission is to help people follow their own story and find their voice so they can help others find theirs. As long as we've embraced our mission, the journey never ends as long as we are alive on the Earth.

Most of us will continue to have identity crises all along the way, but it can be a path marked with growth through the rough terrain of our soul. This journey to your author's voice will help you become more receptive to God, others, and your authentic author voice. Understanding your story will increase the weight of your authority and message to the world, but most of all, if properly evaluated, it can help you rest in who you are without trying to be someone you are not.

In order to uncover your story, you have to learn to tell it in a new way. I want to share an organizational structure to help bring parts of your tale together. Joseph Campbell, an American professor of literature once said, "A hero is someone who has given his or her life to something bigger than oneself"(*Power of Myth*, 1988; p. 123). He specialized in comparative mythology and religion with a focus on the monomyth of the hero, or the "hero's journey." This struc-ture will help you stay on track as you uncover the story of your life. It will help you move from a job to a career, and hopefully to a deeper calling of who you are and who you are meant to serve.

According to the Oracle Education Foundation Library, Joseph Campbell made the hero's journey famous in twelve steps.

1. **Ordinary World**: The hero's normal life at the beginning of the story, before the adventure begins.

2. **Call to Adventure**: The hero faces something that makes him begin his adventure. This might be a problem or a challenge he needs to overcome.

3. **Refusal of the Call**: The hero attempts to refuse the adventure because he is afraid.

4. **Meeting with the Mentor**: The hero encounters someone who can give him advice and ready him for the journey ahead.

5. **Crossing the First Threshold**: The hero leaves his ordinary world for the first time and crosses the threshold into adventure.

6. **Tests, Allies, Enemies**: The hero learns the rules of his new world. During this time, he endures tests of strength of will, meets friends, and comes face-to-face with foes.

7. **Approach**: Setbacks occur, sometimes causing the hero to try a new approach or adopt new ideas.

8. **Ordeal:** The hero experiences a major hurdle or obstacle, such as a life or death crisis.

9. **Reward**: After surviving death, the hero earns his reward or accomplishes his goal.

10. **The Road Back:** The hero begins his journey back to his ordinary life.

11. **Resurrection Hero:** The hero faces a final test where everything is at stake and he must use everything he has learned throughout the journey.

12. **Return with Elixir**: The hero brings his knowledge, or *elixir*, back to the ordinary world, where he applies it to help all who remain there.

Heroes start out as ordinary people, facing tragedies, crises, or irresistible opportunities that push them to go searching for a better life.

Just like in the hero's journey, we must unearth qualities or abilities we never knew we had. I took the stages in the *Power of Myth* (1988) and created a diagram to visualize the journey as you consider your story.

The diagram shows "THE HERO'S JOURNEY" wheel with stages: THE ORDINARY WORLD, THE CALL TO ADVENTURE, THE INITIAL REFUSAL, MENTOR HELPER, CROSSING THE THRESHOLD, TEST ALLIES/ENEMIES, THE APPROACH, THE ORDEAL, THE REWARD, THE ROAD BACK, ATONEMENT, RETURN. Outer ring labels: ADVENTURE CALLS – JOURNEY PREP TIME, ADVENTURE STARTS – PROBLEMS BEGIN, ADVENTURE INTENSIFIES – PROBLEMS GET RESOLVED, ADVENTURE ENDS – THE JOURNEY HOME.

How to Fit the Three Main Stages of a Hero's Journey into the Structure of Your Story

Let's break down the structure and sequence of the hero's journey. I have noticed periods of my life that fit all three stages of the hero's journey. These voices are my *actor* voice, my *achievement* voice, and my *author* voice. Can you place your location in the following three voices I have identified?

Actor Voice

Stage 1: Departure - This is leaving the ordinary world and the call to go on an adventure.

The actor voice is when I was assigned a role early in life by my parents, coaches, and teachers. I followed the rules and boundaries they set for me with a focus on my role as a defensive back, lifeguard, etc.

It's interesting to note that years later, the strict parent, the tough coach, and the most demanding teacher or spiritual mentor were the ones I am grateful for the most in my journey. Those early life stages are really about being an actor and trying on costumes in order to find a place in the world.

Going along with the hero's journey, this is a time of a safe, predictable world stage with rules which one can use to carry out early life duties. This ordinary life is disrupted when he or she gets a call to adventure or a challenge. For example, when Luke Skywalker, from the Star Wars franchise, returned to his farm to find it had been raided by stormtroopers, his aunt and uncle murdered, he is forced to leave. He also saw a vision that Princess Leia was in trouble. It isn't until he meets his mentor, Obi-Wan Kenobi, that he begins to find his purpose to become a Jedi and fight the enemy.

My early departure from home was a combination of following a girl (Tamra) that I thought I needed to rescue—I doubt now if she ever thought she needed to be rescued—and to show my family I could meet the challenge and go on the adventure of being the first college graduate from my family. I wanted to carry the family flag with my own achievements.

Achiever Voice

Stage 2: Initiation - This is when, through the help of mentors or guides, we cross the threshold to face great challenges.

The *achiever voice* is the hero, or heroine, who finds and accepts a new power to defeat what is trying to destroy them and their people. It's a good versus evil type of situation. The hero sets goals to master their new power to help them face tests and trials.

The trial I grew up facing was stuttering, which later proved to be a source of strength when I was called to fight my personal demons. I learned the courage I needed to overcome the embarrassment of my stuttering was the same courage I needed as I shared my story with others about my faith in Christ. My weakness proved to be the strength I needed to outgrow feeling like a misfit. I gained a bigger purpose to rescue people from similar dark moments.

In Star Wars, Luke Skywalker had guides to help him use the Force to defeat Darth Vader. He sharpens his skills to reach his new goals. In the time of trials, he learns how not to be controlled by his emotions, to stop focusing on the inadequacies and negativities, and to commit power within himself. He learns how to be unselfish and let go of loss—the path to the Dark Side.

I could relate to Skywalker because he too was told he would be nothing more than he was. He lacked confidence and let his emotions control him until he met his mentors. He too had to go into the battle even before he was fully trained to handle the Dark Side of the Force.

In the achiever voice of my journey, I raised money, started a campus ministry, and achieved many goals I'd set for myself. I was *saving the world* to prove I could be something, but there was still a part of me that was running with the energy of proving I could be something and not a nobody by being a winner or conqueror.

However, there are times we may do the right things for the wrong reasons. My emotions made me realize I was trying to be someone I was not, and I would never fully get the approval or acceptance I was searching for.

When Luke Skywalker realized his dad was Darth Vader and was tempted by the Dark Side, he faced his biggest obstacle when saving Princess Leia and watching Obi-Wan die in front of him. Luke had to face his greatest fear of not measuring up while confronting the pain of his past.

For me, the largest battle came from the conflict a nd betrayal, which lead me to experience the burning of the "Dark Side." It was a duel between anger and fear or surrender-ing to forgiveness. It was hard to figure out most days which part was winning. It was another level in my heart where I had to face my ego and insecurities. The struggle was between the ego I wanted to both defend and blame, and my true self where I could recognize my own misguided motives in the form of surrendering to my destiny. The pain I can remember that lead to vengeance was a form of "shame." I felt like I had been taken advantage of and left on the field to die. This form of thinking only leads to hate and fear with the potential to hurt us more than the one we are mad at.

My salvation came in the form of surrender when I had to confront my ego's drive for performance recognition. I began to see the part I played in all my successes, losses, failures, and betrayals. I had been wearing a mask, which was hiding both my insecurity and my freedom from seeking others' approval.

So, I began to see my power was in Christ because He strengthens me in my weakness and He cares for me, my friends, and enemies if I have any. In other words, it took more Jedi training to use this new kind of power. I needed to receive the statement "I am enough." I do not need to be someone other than who I am. If I truly wanted my true voice, I needed a resurrection that could only come from more "death" of my troubled inner self.

Jesus said it best in Matthew 16:25, "For if you want to save your own life, you will lose it; but if you lose your life for My sake, you will find it" (NIV).

My last great hurdle, or "death," before moving to greater self-awareness was releasing control of the image I was trying to portray. The initiation stage of the achiever's voice was where I ran toward a career, set goals for the future, faced allies as well as enemies, and confronted my greatest enemy— my personal soul.

All this comes before we can begin the road home toward what I have labeled as the author voice.

Author Voice

Stage 3: Return home

Trials don't end with the transition of the achiever voice driving away from the self-glorying ego. There are more tests ahead, but now the hero or heroine is not the same internally. They carry the gift of victory over the suffering. If we have truly learned from our greatest challenge, we know we have the gift of wisdom to share with others.

In this part of the story, we prayerfully begin to *see by faith*. We can now see our story in a different light and share it in order to find and listen to our true voice. The journey leads toward home, where we will soon be open to the new possibilities we never recognized before.

For example, Luke Skywalker needed to choose between his needs and the greater good. He faced the final battle and destruction of the Death Star in a form of resurrection. Although he wasn't physically reborn, he began to trust the Force and finally grow into his power. His journey helped him mature from a Padawan (apprentice) to Jedi Master.

I am not a preacher. I am telling my story. These things intrigue me. I see the same hero's journey in the life of Jesus. He began his journey as a baby in a manger. He learned from a young age and was crowned as the Chosen One before He began His path to save the world from evil. He proved His power and faced His greatest challenge on trial. He was sentenced to death, giving His life as a ransom for the world, and was in the tomb for three days before He was resurrected.

He then had no limitations, and the limitations He had before were by his own choosing to come as a humble servant and not on a white horse. He gave His followers hope to continue on helping the world and remembering how they were set free through Him. They were now part of His kingdom. They were to live in the power (Force) of His spirit.

Jesus was and still is the King of Kings for me. He has set me free from the prison of myself.

These patterns which can be traced by the hero's journey are a pattern I believe God has given us about Himself and about being made in His image. It is not too hard for me to believe that God created the hero's journey to impact the world.

I have accepted the responsibility to begin my return home, and I am continuing to surrender to the calling of my author voice.

I still struggle with the fear and anxiety of not finishing the return home. I lost so much of myself in battles, and my death has been a slow torture.

One of my biggest fears is not being able to provide for my family the way I want, but I must live by faith. There is a tragic gap between the way life is and the way it ought to be, which causes doubt. I know my ultimate resurrection will be at the return of Christ when he comes on a white horse (Revelations 19:11-16). He takes me home and makes all things new. Until then, I focus on the miniature death of my ego's spiritual resurrection as I grow in God's image on Earth to bring wisdom, gifts, and salvation to my family here.

Each day, I become more liberated in my author's voice. I feel free from needing the world's approval.

The author knows their story and how their story is useful to the world, giving the author greater authority.

CHAPTER 8

The Process to Discover Your Author Voice

*I don't believe people are looking for the meaning of life as much
as they are looking for the experience of being alive.*

JOSEPH CAMPBELL

What does it mean to be alive?
How does one get a sense of aliveness?

The following diagram is my own personal design,
inspired by the steps in the hero's journey. I created the
acronym A.U.T.H.O.R. to organize the steps of your journey
in finding your own voice.

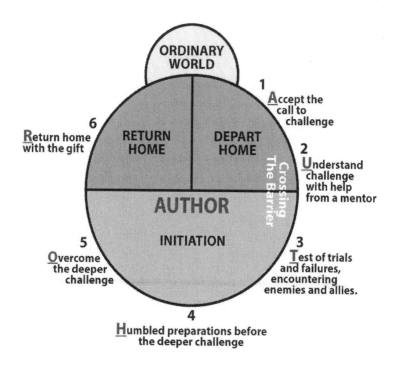

A – Accept

Every beginning begins with the *acceptance* of the call to adventure in order to leave the comfort of home. The call for adventure is the exploratory phase of life that has been awakened by a need, struggle, or challenge. A person must accept the call of the unknown world holding the promise of hope and purpose for one's ordinary life. One must have the courage to venture away from a safe place.

U – Understand

By *understanding* the challenge, we need a guide who can show us how to cross into the unknown world and face the danger. The mentor can give us a kick in the pants to encourage and show us the way. Unfortunately, the mentor can't travel the whole journey with us, so we will have to face the danger alone.

T – Test

A person must encounter a test, find allies, and face enemies while learning the rules of the outside world. This is when one must identify how the ego will act under stress. Events like betrayal can create vengeance and brokenness. Vengeance can be the result of feeling like a victim, whereas brokenness is seeing weaknesses, challenges, and threats as steppingstones to strength and power. Anger leads to a dark path of revenge, while brokenness leads to humility.

H – Humbled

Being *Humbled* is when you discover that your journey is greater than your control. The choice must be made between lying defeated on the road and surrendering to a cause greater than your own existence. A person needs to admit they cannot use their powers to beat the evil, making them powerless. Humility is the admission of a force that can deprive us of our powers. A person will learn to trust and rely on someone or something greater than the self.

O – Overcome

This means we must overcome our very self that is often grounded in arrogance and insecurity. We must release the fear and doubt and embrace both our limitations and our gifts. No one can harm a surrendered soul that has faced the death of the false self and moved to the resurrection of the true self.

R – Return

The *return* highlights the road home. After facing the greatest challenge, the true self gains wisdom, strength, and a cure for the struggle occurring, among others. They gain knowledge of how to save people from the enemy as a reward.

Not everyone is willing to try and understand their journey. In many ways, this process reveals that I'm not only trying to understand how to save my soul but how I could save other people's spirits from depression that causes them to wither. This deeper path toward an author's voice is a pattern to help the light pierce the darkness.

"The light shines in the darkness, and the darkness has not overcome it" (John 1:5 [NIV]).

It's my hope that the more we can picture a developmental life journey, the more we can understand our past, present, and future life of contribution. We will be able to shine our light and see an eternal purpose of God's image in us as well as hope for the future, no matter how dark the situation gets. You can call this a soulful journey, joining a spiritual purpose bigger than ourselves and finding the image of God inside of us.

A is for Accept

The first phase in the A.U.T.H.O.R. process is "accept." Accepting the call to leave home is the first hurdle on the road to adventure. Many young people today seem content to stay near the safety of their parents. However, William Damon, in his book *The Path to Purpose,* says this is because they cannot connect to an "ultimate purpose." He said a big part of the challenge has been "child-centered" or "permissive" parenting. The permissive parent is a parenting style with high responsiveness with very few demands. These parents do not expect mature behavior from their kids, or they are more like a friend than a parent. Because there are few rules, expectations, and demands, children raised by permissive parents struggle with self-regulation and self-control.

We do not help our children if we take the heavy lifting away from them in life. Permissive parenting has been shown to have many negative effects. Relevant points for this book are when children do not have higher expectations on themselves, they drift and become unmotivated, even nihilistic. I am in a personal war against nihilism, the rejection of religious or moral principles in the belief that life is meaningless.

Some children of permissive parents show more aggression and less emotional understanding. If they do not learn to deal with their emotions effectively, they find it hard to deal with situations where they do not get what they want. But the deeper danger comes from the belief that there is no higher source of meaning than themselves and their comfort. There is no cause or ultimate purpose fixed in their mind.

At some point, it's healthy for a young adult to accept the call to leave the safety of home and proceed into the unknown.

Just like in the movies, there's an incident that helps catalyze the call to adventure and risk. For me, it was following a girl to college. The hope of love led me into the unknown, taking me to places of fear and exploration. Some may find a cause to live and sacrifice for, while others might just go along for the ride. The initial drive I had in pursuit of a girl was not life-sustaining.

The acceptance of the call happens during the transition from one's early life to the next. In the ordinary world,

I achieved the status of being an athlete with a cool car and had a few hot dates with girls—or at least that was how I saw it. When I left home, the world became bigger than me. I tried to regain the achievement or image I had in high school, but it fell through, and I had to find a new reason other than a girl and football.

The hero who accepts the call always wants something. In both real life and in movies, characters face transition and instability. The key question to ask is what does hero want?

My younger self believed that going to the University of Arkansas, winning the girl, and being a Razorback football player was what I wanted. The truth is those moments were the early desires or catalyst leading to something bigger, like finding greater meaning and purpose. Inside of those early desires were a form of heroism to save the girl, and make my dad proud of me even if I still stuttered.

Often, the story you construct for yourself is what defines you in the moment. The story that was holding me back was the fear of being no one special as long as I stuttered. I had to find a way to tell a better story for myself, almost like busting a myth. I tried different ways to overcome my image by covering the pain of stuttering with external achievements. At first, I wouldn't accept my weakness as part of who I was, but it was my weakness that eventually led me to the greatest understanding of strength and my true self. Let's say I didn't understand the drive for my performance early on. I only knew I had to accept the challenges that came my way if I was going to be or do anything worthwhile. The acceptance of the challenges was based on a limited awareness of my inner desires and internal struggles. If I had too much awareness early on, I might not have pursued a goal. For instance, if I had known my stuttering was as bad as it was, or if that girl would never love me, I might have sunk into a pit that I have seen many young and older people sink into. It is that early ego protection that is helpful to shield young people from knowing too much too soon about their suffering and weaknesses.

As you identify your story, you first have to ask what it is you want. You must observe yourself from a distance and try to identify your wants.

One way to consider what you want is to ask yourself what is your earliest traumatic childhood memory. This can also give you a clue as to who you are called to serve and what you want to deliver to them. For me the memory was being told by my dad I would never be anything as long as I stuttered. In other words, as long as I stutter I would not have a voice. Part of my calling now is to help people realize their voice in the heart of their challenges. We will ask this question more in the next part on Understanding Your Why.

Questions to consider as you reflect on accepting the call:

1. What are you avoiding, and what is life trying to get you to accept?

2. What limitations make, or made, you fight change?

3. What challenge, opportunity, or struggle pushed you, or is pushing you, to leave the safety of your home?

4. How did your need for independence help you find your calling?

5. How did your dependence on others threaten to keep you from taking responsibility for your life?

Accept the call.

U is for Understand Your Why

Understanding is a big step, but when you combine both internal and external problems, you face a greater challenge. The surface problem for me was a stutter. The day I came to school, kids on the playground lined up and started mocking me.

"C-Ch-Chris—where are you going? D-D-Do—you know?"

The terrible four teased me relentlessly, so much so I felt helpless and ashamed. I felt I didn't have enough strength to tell myself the right messages. I kept telling myself that one day I would show them. I would overcome my stutter.

I handled my external problems by trying to be confident in other things. I would run races against kids on the playground while the older boys would make bets on how well I'd do.

The real question, I had to realize, that was coming from inside of me was:

Do I have what it takes?

This question later in life surfaced, and I had been trying to answer it since my childhood, but the answer was sparked by a book called *Wild at Heart* by John Eldredge (2001). His take on recovering the masculine heart is part of what helped me through the challenges I faced. I feared the failure of not measuring up. Driven by this self-doubt helped me win a lot of foot races on the playground.

When we are driven to prove ourself, no matter how many achievements we make, there is always another hill to climb. The roots to these kind of struggles internally are often found in our insecurity we gained in the early stages of life. For instance, low test scores on the ACT caused me to doubt my ability in academics. The positive side of the drive to prove myself, it helped me endure through a Ph.D., and write this book. But even achievements, winning awards, or having fame can not quench the flame of the nagging question, "Do I have what it takes?"

Do you understand the deeper meaning of your story?

To help you understand your "why" and find your message for the world, I have included a process to help you work through. This process helps uncover how you have b een trying to construct you life and career.

The process is outlined in *My Career Story Workbook* by Savickas and Hartung (2012). This theory and workbook were a large part of my inspiration for this book in the form of Career Construction Theory. There are several other parts of the workbook I don't include here which can provide a more complete picture of your story found in the resources in the back of the book.

I have shared three questions I am using based on identifying your early role models, your favorite saying or motto, and identifying early traumatic childhood memories.

Question 1:

(a) Identify three early heroes or role models you admired.

Be sure to pick three people other than your parents or close friends.

Take some time now to do this.

(b) What did you admire about them?

(c) How are you like them or not like them?

All of us have deep needs. Those needs come from something occurring in our life, often from an early age. The need is often associated with an early challenge or traumatic childhood memory. Remember, my memory was of my dad telling me I would never amount to anything as long as I had a stutter.

This gives clues to the desires and needs that drive me now. One of my core desires is to help people find their voice, authenticity, and authority so they can then help others find their own voice.

The theory of career construction in *The Theory and Practice of Career Construction* (Savickas, M. L. 2005), suggests that we search out heroes and role models who are representations of what we aspire to be in order to overcome the struggles we experience early in life. Savickas suggests early role models represent our idea of ego. Role models are used to comprehend the specific characteristics and qualities a person wishes to use in the attempt to solve a problem.

One hero I really connected with was in the TV series *The Six Million Dollar Man*. The fictional story was about an astronaut and test pilot, Colonel Steve Austin, who was badly injured while testing a plane. Part of the communication between Austin and mission control was saying these words before he crashed and was badly injured. His famous line in the beginning credits has always resonated with me.

"Flight Con! I can't hold it! She's breaking up, she's breaking up—"

Then the rest of the episode is introduced by Oscar Goldman, a government scientist who believed he could save Austin by rebuilding his body with machine parts.

"Steve Austin, astronaut, a man barely alive. Gentlemen, we can rebuild him. We have the technology. We have the capability to build the world's first bionic man. Steve Austin will be that man. Better than he was before. Better, stronger, faster."

When I first heard these words, I was eight years old. Forty-six years later, I still remember them. Austin crashed and was disabled, which was something I passively suffered in my own life. Then someone saw him, believed in him, and repaired him so he could be a hero.

This story helped me with the deeper challenges I was trying to fix. Although fictional, I admired him for overcoming his challenges and finding a way to be better than he was before. At first, Austin couldn't accept he was part machine but later recognized the immense good he could do for other people.

Much of my life journey was and still is about helping people mentally, physically, spiritually, and socially. Something in me identified with Colonel Steve Austin.

When I heard that last line—*"She's breaking up, she's breaking up!"*—it represented the feeling I had when I thought about my stuttering. It was my identity, broken and out of control. I wanted to feel more complete but was trapped in the shell of a cockpit, damaged and in need of repair.

Trapped in my shell, I wanted to be rescued and made whole. I needed to find a purpose for my life.

I also felt inspired by the line "a man barely alive." I wanted to be alive and be known for more than my stuttering voice.

Just like the other line in the show's opening, the government leader insisted Austin could be saved and made more useful. He could be a better man with those enhancements and save the world. Again, the power and hope for a broken, defective man is expressed in this statement:

"Gentlemen we can rebuild him."

I wanted to be rebuilt as Austin had been. I felt defective and wanted to break away from the flaw I believed people saw me to be.

Question 2: What is your favorite saying or motto?

Question two represents the advice you give yourself. According to Savickas, favorite sayings are used to elaborate on your life theme. This can identify your approach to life.

A few quotes from that helped me approach situations from the past, and how I approach life now is still with me today.

One of my favorite quotes is by Robert Jeffress, "The true measure of a man is what it takes to stop him." I had a strong drive to overcome the obstacles I faced from academics and my speech.

Another quote is by C.T. Studd, "If Jesus Christ is God and died for me, then no sacrifice can be too great for me to make for Him." I found my reason to sacrifice and be the man I needed to be.

The last quote that comes to my mind is from the past few years and is credited to Theodore Roosevelt's speech from April 23, 1910. It has been titled "The Man in the Arena."

It is not the critic who counts; not the man who points out how the strong man stumbles, or where the doer of deeds could have done them better. The credit belongs to the man who is actually in the arena, whose face is marred by dust and sweat and blood; who strives valiantly; who errs, who comes short again and again, because there is no effort without error and shortcoming; but who does actually strive to do the deeds; who knows great enthusiasms, the great devotions; who spends himself in a worthy cause; who at the best knows in the end the triumph of high achievement, and who at the worst, if he fails, at least fails while daring greatly, so that his place shall never be with those cold and timid souls who neither know victory nor defeat.

I've had to endure my struggles and battle the reality of failure. I often desired to turn back, unable to find a voice. I was always a people pleaser. I've searched for the courage to step out of my comfort zone and worry less about what people think of me. This is a battle I still fight.

What is your favorite quote? Perhaps, like me, you can remember valuable sayings from different times in your own life.

This next question can be useful in examining a deeper theme of the audience you're meant to serve and the problem you want to cure.

Question 3: What is your most notable traumatic early memory?

Ask yourself what was lacking in your life as a child. Your deep need comes from a struggle, a traumatic experience, or something that made a negative impact.

Identifying this memory can help you voice your meaning and purpose to the world. My struggle was to find a voice since I was a stutterer.

I couldn't figure out my purpose. I would be nothing. I couldn't claim my identity as anything other than through the lens of my "disability." Yet, I still wanted to be more.

I had a deeper need, a need to be seen and heard as someone with value, a need to be recognized as a winner, though I felt like a loser. I knew early on that my dad was not comfortable with me as a stutterer. It was hard for him to wait on me to get my words out, so instead, he refused to listen patiently.

In class, I knew the answer to questions but was too afraid to speak. This caused me to seek attention in other ways just to hide my physical voice.

My passion is helping people discover who they are and how they can serve others. I sought the cure to lacking a voice, and I hope I can help give you the courage to be seen and heard for who you are. I hope to help others find a voice and purpose in their life.

The key is knowing your desires are deeply rooted in the story's narrative of your experiences.

Consider these additional questions to help you understand your why:

1. What are other traumatic childhood memories?

2. What has made you sad, mad, or afraid?

3. What struggles have you had, and how did they create your passion to help others?

T is for Tests

The m ost i mportant p art o f t his j ourney t o fi nding yo ur author's voice is being able to experience a series of tests and failures. This can best be referred to as facing the dark part of your soul or the darkest night of your soul.

After leaving my early mentors when I moved to another state, I had to learn how to live in a new world where no one knew me and my reputation. The *testing* time during your journey is meant to show you what you are truly made of and what you are trusting in. Trials allow us to look deeper into our hearts to understand our real motivations in life.

In all my trials, I've faced darkness, questions, doubts, depression, and anger. Joseph Campbell says,

"It is by going down into the abyss that we recover the treasures of life. Where you stumble, there lies your treasure."
(A JOSEPH CAMPBELL COMPANION:
REFLECTIONS ON THE ART OF LIVING, 1991, pg24)

In the testing times of life, you find out many things you never knew. I used to live in a make-believe world where everyone loved me and wanted the best for me. Though part of that is true, facing relational, financial, emotional, job-related tests helped me discern which inner and outer voices could be trusted. Some of my tests caused me to not trust as much. People often over promise and under deliver.

I heard somewhere that trust is said to relate to your ability to be honest with yourself. Over the years, it's become clear to me that my pain directly resulted from my perception and distrusting myself.

In the Bible, the King of Israel, Solomon, wrote the book of Ecclesiastes, one of the books of wisdom. He saw man's greatest problem wasn't greed or power, but envy. Dan Allender says in *Leading with a Limp* (2006), "Envy comes from a sense of inadequacy and emptiness rooted in wound-edness" (p. 96).

Many leaders have never faced their personal wounds and refuse to rectify the suffering needed to endure the past. They only know comparing or competing with others. A leader who hasn't faced the wounds of the past can become cruel, defensive, arrogant, and emotionally cut off from others. This can lead to narcissism and the desire to be idolized. This is when a leader's much needed confidence can move to arrogance. This happens if the tests in life are not enough to remove the destructive pride blinding us to our own weaknesses and vul-nerability. A friend told me once to never trust a person who cannot cry with you.

Betrayal has been the deepest battle I have faced. When I felt my friends betrayed me, the deepest pain I felt was shame of being abandoned and dismissed. It was as if someone ran over me in my own car and left me on the road to die.

"Feelings of betrayal often come in two forms: abandonment or abuse." A father that promises to play ball with his son but continually doesn't show up cre-ates a feeling of abandonment (Allender, 2006, p.98).

Understanding betrayal and fear of abandonment has helped me better understand my experiences with leaders. From a father wound, brought on early in life by a loving, controlling, raging, protective, and alcohol-addicted father, I believe I often have been drawn to connect to unhealthy leadership out of fear of abandonment and my need for approval. I like this quote because this is the opposite of what a wounded leader does.

"When you recall the people who have influenced you most, you are likely to focus on those that showed acceptance, who encouraged you to find your own voice and whose guidance was accompanied by words of affirmation. You respond best to people whose starting point "I want you to discover what makes you distinct and I want you to lean into that specialness."..........the single most important driver to a life of reliable freedom is having the encouragement to choose your priorities as opposed to being required"

LES CARTER PH.D.

Dan Allender in his book *Leading with a Limp* (2006) says, "When leaders fail to deal with woundedness they fall into envy and oppression." He further states, "Envy comes from a sense of inadequacy, and emptiness rooted in our woundedness" (p. 96).

There is no way to find your authentic voice without dealing with a wounded identity. Life's tests can bring truth to your inner self, which is often accompanied by the statement, "I cannot go on living like this!"

I'd always been an optimistic person. I trusted everyone I met but going through several dark times seemed to destroy my optimism, leading to the metaphorical death of my ego.

The ultimate gift during times of testing is forgiveness.

Forgiveness doesn't always come instantaneously and can still carry the fear of others' abuse and abandonment. It has taken me a long time to release most of my fear and realize I was creating more suffering for myself by not understanding the past. Forgiving, rather than punishing, helped me be honest about my mistakes and the mistakes of others.

If you want to find your author voice, you must identify the testing times in your own journey. Now, it's your time to think deeply about the trials in your life and how they are preparing you for the future.

1. What difficulties, flaws, or weaknesses have tested your commitment?

2. Have you ever been abandoned or abused by someone in authority?

3. What are signs of a narcissist or wound in people around us?

   - Someone not interested in your perspective

   - Someone highly opinionated

   - Someone emotionally detached and impervious to empathy

   - Someone who only cares for what you can produce

4. Is there anyone who helped you stay true to your deeper purpose and meaning?

5. What past offenses do you need to forgive?

6. What profound desires have you become aware of during your tests?

7. How did your own unique gifts help you get through each test?

If you can identify the tests you have faced, you might find the real enemy lurking inside your own heart, and then you might find it easier to forgive yourself and others. You

will see that whatever threatened to harm you has also pro-
vided you strength for the rest of the journey when you let it.

H is for Humbled

*"There is nothing noble in being superior to your fellow man;
true nobility is being superior to your former self."*
— ERNEST HEMINGWAY

Have you ever been humbled to gratefulness? I
define humility as when you can receive a humiliation with
gratefulness. It is a form of surrendering to life's
lesson. Humility has been difficult for me to write
about. Even through all my experiences, I still believe
there is more to be humble about. I think that many
humble people do not see themselves as humble. If they
did, then they would become proud of their humility. I have
not arrived at complete humil-ity because at times, my
own insecurity still tries to claim my rights over others. It
helps to worship a God that came to earth as a servant not
too proud to wash other's feet even when they did not
deserve it.

My path toward humility first involved identifying
or taking ownership of my part in every conflict. I had to
iden-tify how I wanted the power and control driven by fear.
When I finally stopped fighting my experiences and didn't
dwell on revenge, I found a peace that gave me power over
my shame

or anger. I started thinking of myself less and started to accept my role in the conflicts I have had with people in authority.

This s urrendered p eace i s w hat I c all h umility. I c an't say for sure how this peace emerged from my heart, except the more I focused on the hidden longings in my heart, the more I could see the role in my conflicts that I played. I was attracted to people and leaders who were just as wounded as I was. I had to truly forgive those that misunderstood me.

There were emotions that opened the door to my true self: anxiety, fear, depression, and sadness. These emotions warned me that I was living a life that wasn't mine.

I believed seeking out other men who could connect with my brokenness was a form of humility. They helped me get back on the field and believe in myself.

Down the same path to humility, I realized suffering from the actions of others wasn't my biggest problem—it was the way I responded to feeling wronged.

I couldn't control what others did, but I could become more aware of the things my heart desired and the ways I turned away from God to trust in my own self.

In Tim Keller's book, *The King's Cross: The Story of the World in the life of Jesus* (2011, p. 29), he tells of a woman named Cynthia Heimel who was a writer for the *Village Voice*. She wrote an article about struggling actors working in restaurants and punching tickets at theaters to pay their bills before they became famous. Her point was their attitude when they were struggling. They would say things like, "If only I could make it in the business," or "If only I had this or that, I would be happy."

They wanted fame, but it could not satisfy. Keller further quotes Heimel on page 29, about the actors getting the fame they wanted. They became insufferable, unstable, angry, and manic. Not just arrogant, as you might expect—worse than that. They were now unhappier than they used to be.

Keller points out from the Bible that the real problem was building an identity from things that won't last. After reading Keller's book, I realized my real problem was not what happened to me or what people had done to me but how I perceived and responded to each test, which was humbling.

After experiencing a series of tests, it's helpful to remember gratitude negates the "vengeance is mine" type of thinking. Vengeance is only for God to carry out justly.

"Do not take revenge, my dear friends, but leave room for God's wrath, for it is written: 'It is mine to avenge, I will repay,' says the Lord" (Romans 12:19 [NIV]).

Gratitude is the greatest sign of humility at work in our hearts. Gratitude reminds us our new experiences didn't kill us and to be grateful our arrogance didn't kill us, even when it led us into the danger. Gratitude can be a step before or after forgiveness, which comes from humility and surrendering the rights of our old self-ego. Many stories show the hero going after retribution but with more respect for their enemy.

Are you grateful for the tests because they opened the door to forgiving others and yourself in a humble way?

The darkness of the inner cave, gave me time to reflect and prepare for a major battle ahead.

Consider these questions as you look for humility in your growth:

1. What mistakes did you make?
2. How did you handle your most difficult times?
3. What beliefs kept you going during the hard times?
4. How did you evaluate your journey up to this point?
5. How did you overcome taking yourself too seriously?
6. How did you learn to view yourself as one person among many to serve?
7. How did you learn to receive humiliation without losing yourself?
8. In what ways can this reflection make you grateful?

O is for Overcoming Our False Storylines.

All of us have a persona or false storyline we have developed in the first parts of our life. Much of my life has been about trying to please people. I tried hard not to see what really lay beneath my persona of myself. I was a performer. I gained some good applause. Our persona is what we refuse to see about ourselves and what we do not want others to see. Richard Rohr calls our persona our "shadow." Jesus referred to the persona when he said people were, "hearing but not understanding, seeing, but not perceiving" (Matthew 13:14-15 [NIV]). Addicts might call the shadow or persona "denial." It is that part of us that we feel is socially unacceptable and often unwilling to be seen. But to be whole we must overcome the persona or shadow and let the light shine on our false self.

A recent example of my persona happened when I invited a speaker to come to my meeting to speak. I felt this guy was very successful, and my desire was for him to think I was also, or that I, at least, could measure up to him. I wanted him to see the thriving people in my group so he would want to connect with me and the appearance of my success. As authentic as I believe I am becoming, I still have those actor and achiever parts of me that want to please others and make an impression.

Recently, I listened to Jim Carrey's Commencement Address at the 2014 Maharishi University of Management Graduation.

> "Your need for acceptance can make you invisible in this world. Don't let anything stand in the way of the light that shines through this form. Risk being seen in all of your glory."

I think our shadow persona contains our core fears, compulsions, and limitations we wear masks to cover up. When you can name these three enemies of your personality, you will begin to have power over them. We must overcome the contradictions in our life. We must accept that powerlessness, weakness, and failure can become our strength. In the world I grew up in, my shadow was failure, weakness, and shame because success and strength were not associated with those. Richard Rohr, the Founder of the Center of Action and Contemplation, wrote in a daily meditation about the shadow self on September 8, 2019, quoting St. Francis of Assisi, "I will delight in powerlessness, humility, poverty, simplicity, and failure."

Saint Francis of Assisi described this powerlessness, failure, simplicity, and poverty as "perfect Joy." Richard Rohr has written a lot about the shadow and the contradictions we must overcome. The dictionary defines contradiction as, "Two things that cannot both be true, or that are at odds with each other so that if one is correct, the other is not."

This is also known as a paradox, like the premise of this book, Your Obstacle is the Way. The overcoming Richard talks about is a form of surrender. In the story of Jesus, He had to surrender himself to die on the cross. It is hard before surrender to accept the contradiction in us. It is even harder to overcome. Richard Rohr explains the contradiction in his daily meditation blog about the shadow self on September 8, 2019 called Shadow Boxing:

> The larger and deeper shadow for Western individuals and culture is actually *failure* itself. Thus, the genius of the Gospel (Message of Christ) is that it incorporates failure into a new definition of spiritual success. This is why Jesus says that prostitutes and tax collectors are getting into the kingdom of God before the chief priests and religious elders.

The key aspect of the hero's journey is to gain the ability to serve others by surrendering to a form of death, thus leading to resurrection. It is a rebirth from the limitations of flesh and ego. When we are being restored, we can receive a sense of peace after the battle. We can overcome death and be born again once we face and release our fears, compulsions, and limitations but that requires death to our false ego driven self.

Overcoming our struggle is an important part of releasing what we deem important to us, such as our own importance and letting ourselves be seen. We, as humans, tend to cling to what feels important to us. It's referred to as attachment when we fear the loss of what is important to us, like our reputation or persona of success. In my personal faith, I believe God sees me and loves even those areas I found shameful in myself.

For me, overcoming my challenges came from God removing the barriers I'd become attached to like my reputation or my idea. I took criticism as a threat to my status. I resented feeling micromanaged to do staff reports or expense reports, even though much of it was mine to overcome. I might add advice to micromanagers as well. Help people grow in character and not just confidence. I wasn't open to sharing equal ownership of my business idea or process with others, which manifested in my desire to control the situation, becoming angry when I feared others would make me look incompetent. This led to my own experience of betrayal. In his daily reflection blog, Richard Rohr, Saturday, July 16, 2016 wrote: "One of the easiest ways to discover your shadow is to observe your negative reactions to others and what pushes your buttons. Most often, what annoys you in someone else is a trait in yourself that you haven't acknowledged."

The only path to overcoming defeat was to talk about my emotions and overcome the darkness in my heart. I needed to start actually believing the words in Genesis 50:20, spoken by Joseph as he was forgiving others who had betrayed him: "Don't you see, you planned evil against me but God used those same plans for my good, as you see all around you right now—life for many people."

I am not completely sure that anyone ever meant to harm or to betray me. Maybe they were blinded in their own persona. I had to confess that God allowed my pain to happen, but I had to believe He had a purpose for me during my tests. People should not have abandoned me so quickly, but I am now grateful they did because it caused me to write this book and seek my deeper voice from my wilderness experience.

In any good story, the villain is considered the enemy. The true villain in my story was always the feeling that I could not measure up, so I needed to prove my worth. My core derived from shame that caused me to hide from others because my identity was so deeply rooted in fear. Other characters helped me realize how afraid I was to admit to myself that I was my own worst enemy.

I always doubted my abilities, so I constantly searched for external fixes to my insecurity. The core issue was my battle to overcome my fear and limitations and was where my false persona needed to be transformed into a truer self.

Fear-based beliefs must be overcome, compulsions need to be conquered, and limitations have to be beaten through the birth of a deeper and wiser author voice. The fears that have surrounded me throughout my life have been the root of my compulsions to attempt to cover anxiety.

"To him who overcomes I will give some of the hidden manna to eat. And I will give him a white stone, and on the stone a new name is written, which no one knows except him who receives it" (Revelations 2:17 [NIV]). This verse shares the importance of overcoming obstacles. By challenging your problems, you are giving yourself the chance for growth and change. The greater search for truth within yourself comes from overcoming your experiences instead of hiding away and living in fear.

What is your hidden name?

The new name is thought to be the name we will hear when we meet God in the end. I believe when our true name is revealed by God, we will recognize it. It will be the name God claims as His image in us, not a negative earthly name like stupid or stutterer.

If we could only get a glimpse of our new name here on Earth, we would be able to love life and others in a more complete way. This name, only God knows and is the deepest way we bring glory to Him on Earth. It also gives us the power to overcome our trials and adversity.

Perhaps we know it at the soul level. We have to overcome our own flesh and see how small we are compared to God. People who have had a deeply spiritual experience often report seeing the grandeur and beauty of the Divine as well as the humility it brings. It's like swimming in a pond versus the ocean; perspective gives us the chance to recognize our smallness. Life is not about us, and if we try to make it about us, we will live a small life.

The seven deadly sins recognized by Christian teachings are sloth, wrath, pride, envy, greed, gluttony, and lust. Sin is an archery term for "missing the mark." For a Christian, the only power over the deadly sins is grace brought about by the death, burial, and resurrection of Christ.

Atonement for sin based on the Christian religion comes by way of surrender and trust in the work of Christ on the cross. This brings humility to the true believer based on the fact that the penalty for our sins has been placed on Christ. Because of that, the followers of Christ are given what they have not earned, complete forgiveness. The followers of Christ judgment day trial is already over because Jesus stood trial for them. This is grace for Christians to be free to love and give others what they do not deserve.

In my early journey, I believed I was bold, brave, caring, and motivated. I believe these things still exist in me, but the energy that fueled them came largely from insecurity and my need to be unique.

These types of motivations can drive many of your desires if you haven't encountered grace for your soul and found your true source of strength.

If you're lucky, the rumblings of your soul will let you know there's a problem. For me, periods of depression would surface when I wasn't doing what I needed to do to achieve success. I have not arrived yet or completely overcome a lingering sadness that remains. I am comforted as I read the song of King David. David, too, felt a longing as I do for joy in Psalms 42:5:

> Why, my soul, are you downcast?
> Why so disturbed within me?
> Put your hope in God,
> for I will yet praise Him,
> my Savior and my God.

It helps if you know and walk the path back to God and His image, the home of your true identity. Once you have *accepted* the call, you then start to *understand* your external and internal problems. You face *tests* that bring you closer to finding your greatest enemy—yourself. When you recognize these steps, you can then gain *humility* and surrender to your authentic self.

Part of *overcoming* is identifying the good and bad passions inside our hearts.

"Put off the old self, which belongs to your former manner of life and is corrupt through deceitful desires … and put on the new self, created after the likeness of God in true righteousness and holiness" (Ephesians 4:22, 24 [NIV]).

Most everyone can agree there are internal forces that push us in negative directions.

The Enneagram

A helpful tool for personality assessment is the Enneagram. The Enneagram is a model of the human psyche and has been used by many spiritual traditions, including Christians for many years. It's an instrument used to help explain personality types and is based on nine ways of relating in the world.

The Enneagram has helped me identify my behavior as well as my motivations behind the behavior. I suggest using the Enneagram as a tool to look into yourself and the patterns you've been influenced by. It can reveal specific ways you are held captive by yourself as well as the unique ways God intends for you to display His glory and love to the world.

The Enneagram's basic structure is a diagram of nine personality types placed in a circle drawing connection to each type through the roots of spiritual and psychological theories. In the ancient number theory of Pythagoras (500 BC) and equated Christian Mystical ideas, which begin in the Christian doctrine of the seven deadly sins, different sacred traditions of wisdom have contributed to its development.

The idea is to take the sin, passion, or tendency of each type and transform it into its opposite, switching from a negative trait to a positive trait. Just like refocusing from fear to courage, from greed to giving, and from anger to love. The concept refers to your personality as your mask, covering your true self.

Through examining the Enneagram, I learned I am a Type 4, which means my central sin is envying others. I may also dwell on the fact I feel like something is missing in me. I am always in search of my identity. It is as if sadness and emotional pain help me to do my art or writing better. This sort of thinking pattern can make the soul weary and downcast. Knowing my sin of envy and overcoming it with its opposite is my deepest desire.

The Enneagram can help you understand your story better and the way you are trying to operate in the world.

The person credited with the Enneagram system is Oscar Ichazo, born in Bolivia and raised in Peru. He describes nine ways a person's ego becomes fixated within the psyche during the early stages of life. Here is a summary of an interview in 1982 with Oscar Ichazo he describes ego fixations that become the core of a self-image around which their psychological personality develops. Each fixation is also supported at the emotional level by a particular "passion" or "vice." The principal psychological connections between the nine ego fixations can be "mapped" using the points, lines, and circle of the Enneagram figure.

When I'm not centered, experiencing the Grace of God's love in my limitations and strengths, I still fall into lies my inner self creates. I've begun to use the Enneagram lens to help me find my way back home. This tool identifies nine ways I became lost as well as the path I found back to my true self. The purpose of any tool is to seek the understanding of strategies, desires, and motivations developed to navigate your perceived world.

A good first step in experiencing how your limitations and strengths operate in your life is to see how the false self and the authentic self are impacted by stress and growth. The Enneagram personality profile pulls back the curtain of the soul.

Daniel J. Siegel (2010) Clinical Professor of Psychiatry at the UCLA School of Medicine and Executive Director of the Mindsight Institute, says:

> People do have neural propensities—called temperament—that may be somewhat but not fully changeable. No system of adult personality description that exists (except the Enneagram popular version) has an internally focused organization—(pp 2671-2672)

Let's look at some ways this architecture is organized in the Enneagram of personality types from Lyleson (2015, p. 11). It describes the nine basic ways, or temperaments, people try to create and hold onto a sense of self that is deserving of love and happiness; this starts early in childhood.

Type 1: Try to prove what perfect and responsible people they are.

Type 2: Try to prove what indispensable and caring people they are.

Type 3: Try to prove what capable and charming people they are.

Type 4: Try to prove what unique and deep feeling people they are.

Type 5: Try to prove what intelligent and self-sufficient people they are.

Type 6: Try to prove what loyal and non-threatening people they are.

Type 7: Try to prove what happy and positive people they are.

Type 8: Try to prove what powerful and masterful people they are.

Type 9: Try to prove what peaceful and selfless people they are.

The following Enneagram diagram is my own creation, with labels adapted from Dr. Jerome Wagner's *Nine Lenses of the World* (2010), and Wagner's *Spectrum Enneagram* (1996). Each point asks the core question for the coordinating personality to better understand yourself and how to overcome challenges.

THE PEACEFUL PERSON
CORE QUESTION:
How can I focus on people's
agendas and have peace?
• Fear being separated from others.
• Need to avoid and keep balance

THE POWERFUL PERSON
CORE QUESTION:
How can I bring justice and get things
moving in work and play.
• Fear is being controlled by others
• Need to be in control

THE GOOD PERSON
CORE QUESTION:
What is correct or incorrect?
• Fear is imperfection
• Need to be perfect

THE JOYFUL PERSON
CORE QUESTION:
What are my options
and future plans?
• Fear is pain in life.
• Need to experience everything

THE LOVING PERSON
CORE QUESTION:
How can I meet other's needs.
• Fear disappointing and being unloved by others
• Need to be liked

THE LOYAL PERSON
CORE QUESTION:
What could go wrong?
• Fear that everything will go wrong.
• Need to be safe and sure

THE EFFECTIVE PERSON
CORE QUESTION:
How can I achieve recognition
for accomplishments?
• Fear is being rejected or not valued.
• Need to win and all cost

THE WISE PERSON
CORE QUESTION:
How can I get understanding
and knowledge?
• Fear being useless and incompetent.
• Need to understand everything

THE ORIGINAL PERSON
CORE QUESTION:
What is missing in me?
• Fear being abandoned, defective, and misunderstood.
• Need to be special or unique

R is for Remedy

R is for both *remedy* and the *return home*. If you have done the work, you will have a remedy for the people you mentor when you return home.

On the hero's journey, after surviving your greatest challenge, you now possess the treatment for your world's needs.

The hero's reward is the potion or remedy for a world in need gained from the battle (great Ordeal) they have survived.

At the time of writing this, I'd just attended a self-help meeting for men who struggle with things like drug addictions, divorce, gambling, etc. I identified myself as a member of this group with similar struggles in the hopes of continuing to grow in finding my authentic voice.

During a meeting, one of our regular members came in with a young man. Let's call him John. At first, I didn't recognize him, but when he introduced himself, I real-ized I knew him from seven or eight years ago. John was a friend of my son's, and we had some big adventures together when he was younger. He was pale and thin from his drug addiction.

When he shared his story with the group, I got emo-tional. I told him I loved him and that I wanted him to know he wasn't alone. My emotion came from realizing my obsta-cles were the remedy needed to help John. My past suffering prepared me to be right there in that room for that moment when this young man needed to see he was not alone in his struggle.

With John, I saw the importance of my struggle, to be useful to my world. Helping John with his addiction further clarified that it was my past battles that made helping him possible.

Frederick Buechner, American writer, novelist, poet, autobiographer, essayist, preacher, and theologian said in his book *Wishful Thinking*, "Vocation - The place God calls you to is the place where your deep gladness and the world's deep hunger meet" (p. 95).

The definition of *vocation* begins with the self and travels toward the needs of the world. My suggestion, if you are looking for vocation, is to begin with the world's deep need that you see and look for the cure you have acquired in your personal battles that you have overcome.

The bottom line is every need in the world does not have your name on it. You are harming the world when you neglect your true voice and try to be someone you are not. The ultimate purpose of this book, like Buckner said, is to help you get to where your deep gladness meets the world's deep need. It is my hope that your struggle can be used as a remedy for your world.

In his book *The Road to Charter* (2015), David Brooks says pride is "building your happiness around your accomplishments, using your work to measure your worth." The thought of working hard and playing by the rules which can help you find a *good life* is the source of many young people's desperation and many middle-aged people's disappointed depression. Brooks further adds, "The problem, Augustine came to believe, is that if you think you can organize your own salvation you are magnifying the very sin that keeps you from it. To believe that you can be captain of your own life is to suffer the sin of pride" (p.198-199).

My remedy wasn't to be found in my performance or in being a savior, but when I was forced to my knees in defeat. Only then could I see a bigger story and purpose.

St. Augustine, a fourth-century philosopher, was known for laying the foundation for much of Western Christianity. He wrestled between his desire for self-absorption and his desire for moral perfection. His inner morals battled his great mind as he tried to focus on the pleasures of the world over the pleasures of faith. He finally concluded the path to true joy wasn't through control and performance, but through surrender and being receptive to Christ. One of the first parts Augustine read in the Bible: "Not in carousing and drunkenness, not in sexual excess and lust, not in quarreling and jealousy. Rather, put on the Lord Jesus Christ, and make no provision for the desires of the flesh" (Romans 13: 13-14 [NIV]).

He describes the experience of Christ's love as a light flooding his soul, taking away the shadow. He found the cure, which was a higher love and purpose above worshiping himself.

Have you found a higher love?

Have you found the remedy to serve the people of your world?

CONCLUSION

Once you've asked yourself the important questions in this book, you can begin to see facets of your story that could make it better. Through the A.U.T.H.O.R. process, you can learn from your stories, role models, hero's journey, and even the Enneagram to map where you have been and be confident in where you are now.

In Stephen Covey's *The 8 th Habit* (2004), he explains the concept of how to "find your voice and inspire others to find theirs." (p. 5). Covey suggests that your voice is "your unique personal significance—significance that is revealed as we face our greatest challenges and which makes us equal to them"(p. 5).

That is my desire for this book. To provide a roadmap to discover your story and unique ability to go through suffering and pain to true fulfillment, in taking the responsibility you were meant to carry. Don't let the world beat your story into its own mold. Find your Author Voice and inspire others to find theirs.

REFERENCES

1. *Holiday, R. (2014)* ***The Obstacle Is the Way: The Timeless Art of Turning Trials into Triumph. Porfolio (US)***

2. Brown, B. (2012). *Daring greatly: How the courage to be vulnerable transforms the way we live, love, parent, and lead.* New York: Spiegel & Grau.

3. Clifton, J. (June 13, 2017). The World's Broken Workplace. The Chairman's Blog. https://news.gallup.com/opinion/chairman/212045/world-brokenworkplace.aspx?g_source=position1&g_medium=related&g_campaign=tiles

4. Brown, B., 3 Things You Can Do To Stop a Shame Spiral: Opra's Life Class, Opra Winfrey Network, YouTube October 6, 2013

5. Palmer, P. J. (2000). *Let your life speak: Listening for the voice of vocation.* San Francisco: Jossey-Bass.

6. Allender, D.: Spiritual Abuse, Part One by The Allender Center on March 2, 2018

7. Henriques, G. Why Is It So Hard for Some Men to Share Their Feelings? Nov 13, 2014 Blog in Psychology Today

8. Bates, Laura (16 April 2013). "The Everyday Sexism Project: a year of shouting back". *The Guardian*. Retrieved 26 January2016.

9. Brooks, David (2015-04-14). The Road to Character (pp. 198-199). Random House Publishing Group. Kindle Edition.

10. Damon, W. (2008) The Path to Purpose: How Young People Find their Calling in Life. New York: The Free Press.

11. Dweck, Carol S. (2016). Mindset: The New Psychology of Success (p.6). Penguin Random House Publishing.

12. *Eye of the Tiger* (album), the 1982 album by Survivor

13. Campbell, j. (1991) *A Joseph Campbell Companion: Reflections on the Art of (PG 24)*

14. Rohr, R. (2011). *Falling upward: a spirituality for the two halves of life.* San Francisco: Jossey-Bass

15. Howes, L. [The School Of Greatness]. (2017, September 12). Brené Brown: Create True Belonging and Heal the World. [video].

    Retrieved from https://lewishowes.com/podcast/r-brene-brown-create-true-belonging-and-heal-the-world/

16. Keller, T. J., & Alsdorf, K. L. (2012). *Every good endeavor: Connecting your work to God's work.* New York: Dutton.

17. Vess, L., Lara, T. (2015) Career Counseling and Family Therapy: An Interview with Mark Savickas, PhD

18. Palmer, P. J. (2000). *Let your life speak: Listening for the voice of vocation.* San Francisco: Jossey-Bass

19. Collins, J. C. (2001). *Good to great: Why some companies make the leap ... and others don't.* New York, NY: Harper Business

20. STAY ON THE BUS is excerpted from the commencement speech at delivered at the New England School of Photography in June 2004

21. Campbell, J., & Moyers, B. D. (1988). *Joseph Campbell and the power of myth with Bill Moyers.* New York, NY: Mystic Fire Video

22. Eldredge, J. (2004). *Wild at heart: Discovering the secret of a man's soul.* Waterville, Me: Walker Large Print

23. Miller, D., & OverDrive Inc. (2017). *Building a storybrand: Clarify your message so customers will listen.* [New York]: HarperCollins Leadership, an imprint of HarperCollins

24. *Savickas M., Hartung (2012) My Career Story Workbook* (2012) http://www.vocopher.com/mcsu/MCS_26_GIUGNO%20 (1).pdf

25. Savickas, M. L. (2005). *The Theory and Practice of Career Construction.* In S. D. Brown & R. W. Lent (Eds.),*Career development and counseling: Putting theory and research to work* (p. 42–70). John Wiley & Sons Inc.

26. Campbell, J. (1991) *A Joseph Campbell Companion: Reflections on the Art of Living*, 1991

27. Allender, D. (2006). Leading with a Limp; Waterbrook press; A division Of Random house.

28. Neider, L., Schriesheim, C. (2010) *The Dark Side of Management* p. 29

29. Keller, T. (2011). Kings Cross: Story of The World in the Life of Jesus. Penguin Group

30. Blog by Richard Rohr Shadow Boxing Sep 8 2019

31. Ichazo, Oscar (1982). *Interviews with Óscar Ichazo*. Arica Press. ISBN 0-916554-02-3.

32. Siegel, Daniel J., (2010) *The Mindful Therapist, A Clinician's Guide to Mindsight and Neural Integration*, New York: W. W. Norton & Co kindle (pp. 2671 -72)

33. Lyleson, E. (2015) Essential Wholeness: Integral Psychotherapy, Spiritual Awakening, and the Enneagram. Balboa Press: A division of Hay house.

34. Wagner, J. (2010). Nine Lenses of The World: The enneagram Perspective.

35. Wagner, Jerome. The Enneagram Spectrum of Personality Styles. Portland, Or: Metamorphous Press, 1996.

36. Buechner, F. (1973). *Wishful thinking: A theological ABC*. New York: Harper & Row.

37. Brooks, David (2015-04-14). The Road to Character (pp. 198-199). Random House Publishing Group. Kindle Edition.

38. Eagleman, D. [Big Think]. (2018 year, August 5th). How the mind makes new ideas: Bending, breaking, blending [Video file]. Retrieved fromhttps://www.dailymotion.com/video/x6rgjku

39. Covey, S. (2004). The 8th Habit: From Effectiveness to Greatness. Free Press